A SOLDIER AND A

A SOLDIER AND A GENTLEMAN

The life of
BRIGADIER GENERAL
SIR BERTRAM PERCY PORTAL
K.C.B., D.S.O.
1866-1949

RICHARD WALDRAM

Matador
9 Priory Business Park,
Wistow Road, Kibworth Beauchamp,
Leicestershire. LE8 0RX
Tel: 0116 279 2299
Email: books@troubador.co.uk
Web: www.troubador.co.uk/matador
Twitter: @matadorbooks

ISBN 978 1803130 095

British Library Cataloguing in Publication Data.
A catalogue record for this book is available from the British Library.

Printed and bound in Great Britain by 4edge Limited
Typeset in 12pt Adobe Garamond Pro by Troubador Publishing Ltd, Leicester, UK
Cover design by the author: Bertram Portal, by kind permission of the family.

Matador is an imprint of Troubador Publishing Ltd

If this book makes any profits they will be donated to
Overton charities and organisations.

COVER PHOTOGRAPH

It is not known exactly when this photograph of Bertram was taken but he appears to be about forty at the time when he was colonel of the 17th Lancers in India. He did not have an imposing physical presence. He was 5ft 9in tall and weighed 10 stone, the ideal physique for a cavalryman. Look at the eyes. Bertram was thoughtful, observant, intelligent, capable, adaptable and decisive. He was also a kindly man who took great care of his men and their horses and endeared himself to all who knew him.

MONEY

In Bertram Portal's lifetime the £ was divided into 20 shillings, abbreviated to 's.' and there were 12 pennies or pence to a shilling, abbreviated to 'd.' from the Latin *denarius*.

Conversion to today's values is fraught with difficulty and has not been attempted in this book. Some comparison can be made by reference to an agricultural labourer's basic weekly wage which was about 12s. in 1880, 17s. in 1914 and about £5 in 1939.

Source: British Labour Statistics: Historical Abstract 1886-1968
(Department of Employment and Productivity, 1971)

CONTENTS

FOREWORD

I have lived in Overton in north Hampshire for 46 years, less than half a mile from Southington House which was Bertram Portal's home. One of his granddaughters lived at the house for much of this time and is a family friend. In the process of research for a book about the history of Overton, I discovered a great deal about Bertram Portal and became convinced that his life story deserved to be better known.

He wrote his own account of his early life and often kept diaries, most of which have survived. His children and grandchildren kept his records and letters and deposited hundreds of them in various archives.

He was a true gentleman – honourable, courteous, considerate to all and modest about his achievements. He was guided throughout his life by his faith and had a strong sense of duty but seemed to enjoy everything he did. He was a very successful polo player and a keen huntsman. Above all he was a family man and their story is woven into the narrative of this book. Apart from his military exploits as a cavalryman, he played a prominent role in the village of Overton and the County of Hampshire, as did his father and other members of the family for over 150 years.

He led an eventful life spanning a period of immense military and social change. Trained to fight on horseback with sword and lance, he lived to see the use of nuclear weapons.

ACKNOWLEDGEMENTS

I was very pleased to find that his grandchildren and a great-nephew shared my enthusiasm for this project. They ransacked their cupboards and kindly allowed me to photograph the many letters and images still in their possession. This book is very much richer as a result and I am most grateful to all of them. They are Joanna Durham Matthews, Simon and Robert Portal, Sir Jonathan Portal, Hyacinthe and Henry Harford, Desmond Longfield, Angus Macintosh, Mark Litchfield and Elizabeth Bamford.

I am also most grateful to Sir Michael Salt, grandson of Sir Thomas Salt, staff officer to Bertram Portal during and after the Easter Rising in Dublin, for permission to quote extracts from his grandfather's diary.

It is a pleasure to record my thanks to Valerie Joynt, Alison Deveson and Hyacinthe Harford who all made critical appraisals of my draft and saved me from making some ghastly errors. I am particularly grateful to Dr Jonathon Boff, Reader in the History of Warfare at the University of Birmingham, for appraising the draft, correcting a number of military points and for his helpful suggestions which I have included in the text. Any remaining mistakes are my own.

I am also most grateful for the excellent service I have received at the National Archives at Kew, Hampshire Archives, the National Army Museum, the Imperial War Museum, the British Library, Trinity College Dublin Library and the National Archives of Ireland despite all the difficulties caused by the corona virus.

Richard Waldram
October 2021

CHAPTER 1

EARLY LIFE,
1866 – 1885

Bertram Percy Portal was born on 10th January 1866 at Malshanger House in north Hampshire, a large country house set in about 400 acres of parkland, six miles west of Basingstoke and east of Overton,

Fig. 1. Malshanger House.

Laverstoke and Whitchurch.[1] The family also rented a London town house at Eaton Square in Belgravia where they employed 13 servants including two governesses and a nurse.[2] Bertram was born into a wealthy family.

His forebears had played a prominent role in Hampshire over four generations. Henri Portal was a young French Huguenot who fled persecution after the revocation of the Edict of Nantes, arriving at Southampton in about 1706. He found an influential community of Huguenot émigrés with whom he became involved, working in a paper mill at South Stoneham, near Southampton, in about 1710. In 1712 Portal set up a small paper mill at Bere Mill, Whitchurch and in 1718 he bought the lease of Laverstoke Mill. He secured a contract with the Bank of England to supply high-quality paper for bank notes and the profits led to his acquisition of Freefolk Manor nearby.[3]

When Henri died in 1747 he was succeeded by his son Joseph who was establishing himself in the county. In those days, the road to social and political influence lay in buying land. Joseph bought the Laverstoke Estate in 1759 and by 1763 he was High Sheriff of Hampshire.

When Joseph died in 1793, his son John Portal inherited the paper business. His elder brothers, William and Harry, inherited the family estates but they both died childless. At this time the estates would have been regarded as a more valuable asset than the business, both in terms of the potential profit and that it was not thought well of to be 'in trade'. Harry built a new Palladian mansion at Laverstoke Park in 1798.[4] John Portal invested the profits from the paper business in land. By 1847, he held 84% of the land in Overton parish, including all 13 farms which he let to tenant farmers.[5]

At his death in 1848, the estates were inherited by his eldest son Melville who owned 10,966 acres in Hampshire.[6] He became an MP, was appointed High Sheriff of Hampshire in 1863 and was a Justice of the Peace.[7] John's second son, Robert, achieved fame by surviving the charge of the Light Brigade at Balaclava. He later became colonel of the 5th Lancers.[8] The third son and Bertram's father, Wyndham Spencer, was educated at Harrow School and graduated from Sandhurst but was judged to have a weak heart and was therefore given the paper business.[9]

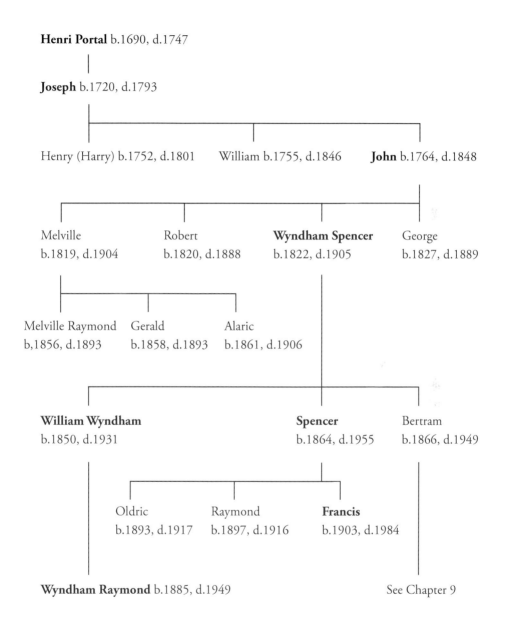

Simplified Portal family tree showing only those of the male line who are mentioned in the text. Those most closely associated with the paper mills are shown in bold.

He stood for Parliament as a Liberal but was unsuccessful. He was a J.P. and became deputy Lieutenant of Hampshire.[10]

The family were much involved in the welfare of local people. Bertram's father was particularly concerned about the evils of drunkenness amongst the labouring classes and the promotion of temperance. He provided 24 acres of land in Overton as allotments for a nominal rent and inaugurated the Overton Branch of the Hampshire Friendly Society in 1851.[11] Wyndham was president of the Overton Reading Society from 1853 though it proved to be short-lived.[12] He was treasurer of Overton's National School from 1844 and supported it financially.[13] In 1869 he wrote a paper entitled 'The poor and how to help them', addressed to the major landowners of Hampshire.[14] Bertram's uncle Robert started the Overton Working Men's Club in 1871 which endured.[15] His uncle Melville was chair of Overton Cricket Club from 1851 and he also supported the National School.[16]

Bertram's father, and indeed the whole family, clearly believed that *noblesse oblige*. They were blessed with wealth, position and influence and lived in some style but took their obligation to help those less fortunate very seriously.

Fig. 2. Bertram.

These then were the influences on Bertram's young life. He sang a solo at the Overton Working Men's Club when he was 13.[17] When he was seven, the family called him 'Old Fats'. This might have been a statement of fact but it is more likely to have been ironic because he was skinny.[18] When Bertram was born his eldest brother William Wyndham was already 16 whilst Spencer was 1½. Spencer and Bertram became the closest companions.

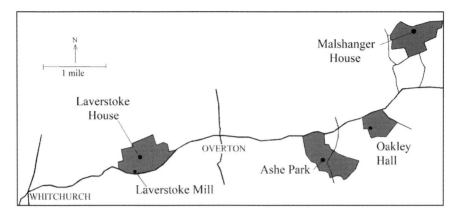

Map 1. The Portal family homes and Oakley Hall in the Test Valley, c.1875.

When Bertram was young he made close and enduring bonds with his cousins and the extended family. His uncle Melville and family lived at Laverstoke and uncle Robert lived at Ashe Park. His uncle George, a clergyman, lived at Burghclere and his mother's family lived at Oakley Hall. His oldest sister, Constance, married William Kingsmill who lived at Sydmonton, near Kingsclere. His second sister, Eleanor, married Chaloner Chute who lived at the Vyne, Sherborne St. John. The Kingsmills and the Chutes were long-established, prominent Hampshire families. All of these relatives had children and sizeable houses where they could host big family parties.

We are very fortunate that in later life, Bertram wrote an account of his childhood memories which he entitled, 'A Link with the Past'.[19] It provides a lively description of the life of a gentry family in the mid-Victorian era.

A LINK WITH THE PAST

We had a wonderfully happy childhood at our home at Malshanger, my father, mother and seven children. They were Constance, Eleanor, Willie, Minnie, Eveline, Spencer and myself. My brother Willie was 16 years older than me and my brother Spencer 1½ years older so we were thrown very much together.

We all worshipped our parents. My father was a very handsome man, 6ft high and full of energy and general knowledge. From his early days he was tremendously keen about the administration of the Poor Law and was for a great number of years Chairman of the Board of Guardians at Basingstoke and Whitchurch. He took early to railway work and was a Director and then Chairman of the old London & South Western Railway… He was also very keen on 'thrift' and for very many years was President of the Hampshire and General Friendly Society which made great progress under his supervision. He considered the chief cause of crime was drunkenness and he attended many temperance meetings in London and elsewhere and a great number of Temperance Fetes were held in the park at Malshanger. He was not a total abstainer himself and enjoyed a glass of wine. After one of his meetings it was pointed out to him that his words would carry more weight if he said that he himself was a teetotaller; he promptly took the pledge at the age of about 60.

He was a very keen churchman and spoke at several Church Congresses which used to be held annually. He greatly objected to any relaxation of the 4th Commandment.[20] He was also devoted to trees and flowers and was a keen geologist.

My mother was a daughter of Col. Beach of Oakley and was a very delicate child, with threatening of lung trouble. When she married, people said how sad it was that there seemed little chance of the lovely Miss Beach being able to live for more than a few years. She lived to celebrate her golden wedding surrounded by children and grandchildren. She was, however, always delicate and lived a quiet life. Her influence with all of us was wonderful. Her word was always final and there was never any idea of questioning or argument. She was clever, with a great knowledge of history and was also gifted with a wonderful memory. In her later years she frequently recited poetry, either in our home circle or after a dinner party, to the great enjoyment of her listeners and to the great delight of my father. She was never able to go on expeditions but always encouraged our father to take us which he was always ready to do. She had a great sense of humour, a deep religious faith and was a great influence for good amongst her family and friends.

MALSHANGER

We had numerous relations and friends in the neighbourhood of whom we saw a good deal. My Father's eldest brother Melville lived at Laverstoke and his second brother Col. Robert lived at Ashe Park.

My earliest recollection is a visit to Malshanger of the Bishop of Winchester, Samuel Wilberforce. My brother Spencer (age 6) and I (age 4) stood on either side of the front door, each of us holding a small flag. If the Bishop shook hands with us, we were instructed to say 'How do you do, my Lord Bishop'. Everything appeared to work according to plan but Spencer declared that I had spoilt it all and that I had greeted the Bishop with, 'How do you do, my Lord Pea Soup!' Quite untrue.

There was a turnpike gate across the road just east of the crossroads on the way to Basingstoke.[21] It often made a tiresome delay but it was not an unfair toll. The only method of repairing the road was by laying down cartloads of flints to the severe detriment of the paint on the wheels of carriages. My father frequently used Basingstoke Station for trains to Winchester and London and sometimes a message came from the stables, while we were at breakfast, to say that the carriage must start 10 minutes early as flints had just been laid. The horses could only go at walking pace and a footman had to be ready with a hoof-pick to pick out the sharp flints which would invariably get embedded in the horse's frog.

The headmaster of our private school at Farnborough was a great Etonian and insisted that all the boys should wear top hats on Sundays. No games were allowed but when the weather was fine we always went for country walks, walking in twos, all in top hats and accompanied by masters. Sometimes we walked through some rather whiffy farms and the order was given 'spit boys, spit' which was supposed to prevent any infection.

BERTRAM   SPENCER

Fig. 3. Bertram and Spencer

While we were at Farnborough there was an epidemic of diphtheria and the boys were sent away. The Lodge at Malshanger was prepared for us and our dear old nurse came to look after us and we thoroughly enjoyed ourselves. We had our ponies and were able to ride over the country, but not allowed into any house. The nurse, Westhorpe, came when my brother Willie was a baby and stayed at Malshanger till she died. Her wages were, I believe, £35 a year. She saved money every year and my father advised her on the investment of it. She always insisted on slipping ten shillings into my pocket when I went off to school. When she died she left about £500 to be divided between me and my brothers and sisters! I bought a gold watch chain with a portion of it.

It was while we were at Farnborough that my grandmother died and was buried at Laverstoke. It was arranged that Spencer and I were to attend the funeral. We found our way to Farnborough station arrayed in Eton jackets, black trousers and top hats. When the train arrived there was a large saloon carriage full of black coated gentlemen among whom was my father. At Overton station there were several carriages and we all drove to Laverstoke House where we were all asked for our hats which were then enveloped in crepe streamers. Ours were rather long and nearly touched the ground and we were perfectly delighted with them. A sitting room down stairs was hung with purple hangings. The coffin was placed on a sort of bed and there were masses of tall wax candles and a profusion of flowers, all very impressive. Presently the names of those present were called out and a procession was formed, all walking in pairs. Spencer and I walked together to the mortuary chapel where the funeral service was held and the coffin lowered into the family vault.[22]

The great event at Christmas was the annual children's dance at Oakley Hall. It was the only house in the neighbourhood where there were footmen in livery with powdered heads and knee breeches and white stockings and we looked at them with great admiration. If any ladies came to stay they always brought their lady's maids with them and they always had to sit up till their mistresses returned from dances sometimes at 3 or 4 o'clock in the morning and they had to keep up the fires in the bedrooms.

We had ponies at an early age and much enjoyed hunting with the Vine Hounds of which my uncle William Beach was the Master. All the neighbourhood used to hunt and there were plenty of foxes. We often went out from Malshanger, my father, one of my sisters and Spencer and I, on our ponies. There used to be 'Lawn meets' at the big houses at which a huge breakfast was supplied for all those hunting and cherry brandy for the huntsman and whips, after which riders became very bold!

During the holidays one of the things Spencer and I enjoyed most was to ride to Sydmonton Court, a lovely ride of about seven miles across the Downs. We always received a warm welcome from my sister

Constance. We also often stayed there where we revelled in the bath room, which was the only one we had ever seen. At Malshanger there was no bath room and when the house was full, which it frequently was, baths in the winter were placed before a roaring coal fire with large cans of hot water. The lighting of the house was, of course, entirely by candles and lamps.

Just before midnight on New Year's Eve the whole family, including all the servants, assembled in the dining room for short prayers, read by my father, asking for God's blessing on the coming year. It was a very impressive gathering. There were generally over 50 people, including servants, sleeping in the house for the New Year party.

Our church at Oakley was just 1½ miles away. We often went twice in the day. Tall hats were invariably worn on Sundays. The service took at least 1½ hours and the sermon about 45 min. I remember when surplices were introduced at our church at Church Oakley. The agricultural labourers, who used to attend in their smock frocks, thought it was terribly Popish! The ordinary agricultural labourer's wage in those days was 12 shillings a week. People lived very cheaply and there were no means of getting about except by train or bicycle, nor were there any cinemas. 'Penny readings' were held in the villages and greatly appreciated. We all took part in them.[23]

LONDON

In the Spring of 1872 we were in London. The Prince of Wales had just recovered from a very dangerous illness and there was a great public thanksgiving service at St. Paul's Cathedral. The procession started from Buckingham Palace. One of the Police Commissioners was a friend of my father's and my brother Spencer and I were put under his charge for viewing the procession. My brother happened to be just the same age as Prince Eddie (the elder brother) and I was just the same age as Prince George (afterwards George V). As we were being conducted to our seats by the Police Commissioner, someone in the crowd said 'There go the young princes!' and this caused a considerable stir, to our great delight.

We should not have dreamt of going to London, even in the day, except in top hats. When my brother and I were both at a school in Farnborough we made a day trip together to London, where my parents had taken a house. We went by train and got out at Vauxhall, which everyone did who wanted to go to the West End. The roads in London were bad and very muddy, and at all important crossings there were sweepers who earned considerable money. The streets were very badly lit by oil lamps. The lamplighter had to light them as quickly as possible. He carried a short ladder which he put up against the lamp post. He ran up it, lit the lamp and then ran full speed to the next lamp post.

The street organ-grinder was always a great delight to us children. He was almost invariably an Italian and had a small, wistful looking monkey sitting on the organ. They frequented the West End and played the popular tunes of the day. No 'exeat' to London was complete without a visit to Gunters in Berkeley Square where you were supplied with a most luscious strawberry cream ice for the exorbitant price of one shilling.

It was also customary in London to give evening 'At Homes' to which people went after dinner, arrayed in their best clothes. It was also the custom to drive to Hyde Park in the evening, after tea. The road from Hyde Park Corner to Kensington was packed with carriages, one line going East and the other line going West. A space was kept by police between the two lines and there was great excitement when a policeman was seen trotting between the lines, which meant that a royal carriage was coming, generally containing the Princess of Wales looking perfectly lovely. Queen Victoria was hardly ever seen.

Bertram recalled the activities of his family but also devoted much attention to the lives of very ordinary people – the lady's maids, the

*Fig. 4. Bertram
in a school house
photograph, aged 14.*

footmen, the lamplighters, the street sweepers and the agricultural labourers. He was brought up to be considerate to others and he remained so throughout his life.

Bertram's father evidently intended him to have a military career, since he was the youngest of three sons and could not expect to inherit the family estates or the paper mill. He was sent to Wellington College, which had been opened in 1859 near the Royal Military College at Sandhurst with the intention of supplying the College with suitable cadets.

The school magazines show that Bertram started in 1879 when he was 13. He did well at cricket as a bowler and also at half-back at rugby though he did not play for the school in either sport. He did not receive any academic prizes but appeared in two plays on Speech Day in 1883 in the title role of Shakespeare's Richard II and in a play by Molière performed in French.[24]

ROYAL MILITARY COLLEGE, SANDHURST

Bertram passed the entry examinations and started the course in December 1884 at the age of 18½. Most of the 'gentlemen cadets' were the sons of officers and came from the public schools. The cost was £40-£80, those of higher rank paying more. Bertram's father was described as a 'Private Gentleman' and had to pay the top rate of £125. There was also a charge of £35 for uniforms and books.[25]

The course was eminently practical. Indoor book work formed only a small part of the training but included knowledge of guns, defences, bridges, military history, map reading, topography and tactics. The assumption behind all the training was that the British Army would face a uniformed national army in battles of manoeuvre in open country.

They also had to learn military law and the Queen's regulations and had tuition in French and German.

The theories explained in the lecture halls were put into practice in the field, and parties of cadets could be seen on all fine mornings hard at work digging shelter trenches, throwing up field works, bridging and sketching. The afternoons were principally devoted to rifle practice, sword drill, riding and signalling. Physical training included gymnastics, swimming, football, cricket, tennis, fives and athletics every afternoon.[26] Cadets were not allowed to keep a horse, to play polo or to hunt on the College estate.[27]

Winston Churchill, who was a near contemporary, recalled,

> Discipline was strict and the hours of study and drill parades very long. The practical work in field fortification was most exciting. We made up primitive landmines; we cut up railway lines with slabs of guncotton and learned how to blow up masonry bridges and make pontoons. We drew contoured maps of all the hills round Camberley, made road reconnaissance in every direction, set out picket lines and plans for advance guards. I was very tired at the end of the day.[28]

In the riding school they learned mounting and dismounting a bareback horse at a trot or a canter; jumping a high bar without stirrups or saddle with hands clasped behind the back and jogging at a fast trot with nothing but the horse's hide between the knees. It brought the inevitable falls.[29]

In the final examinations, Cadet B. P. Portal scored 2090 marks which was described

Fig. 5. Lt B. P. Portal after graduation in the uniform of the 17th Lancers, 1885.

Fig. 6. Cap badge of the 17th Lancers.

as 'good' but not 'very good'. He was not a high-flyer but it was respectable. He followed in his uncle Robert's footsteps as a cavalryman by receiving a commission to the 17th Lancers in August 1885.[30] This was a fashionable regiment nicknamed 'the Death or Glory Boys', a reference to their motto which was adopted long before the Charge of the Light Brigade. Officers in this regiment had a reputation to uphold.

CHAPTER 2

YOUNG OFFICER,
1885-1899

LUCKNOW

In October 1885 Bertram sailed to India to join the garrison of the 17th Lancers at Lucknow, lying in the plains 300 miles south east of Delhi.[1]

At this time the British Indian Army was composed of the armies of the three presidencies of Bengal, Madras and Bombay, the presidencies being a left-over from the days of the East India Company. In 1858 the Crown took control of India from the Company after the Indian Mutiny the year before. The function of the three armies was to deter or control civil unrest. In 1887 there were 31 garrisons across the sub-continent.[2] They consisted of British infantry and cavalry regiments, or battalions thereof, sent in rotation from Britain as well as Indian regiments with British officers. The tour of duty in India for British regiments was generally four years.

Winston Churchill described the life of a subaltern in India at about the same time.

The pay was 14 shillings a day with about £3 a month to keep two horses. No quarters were provided for the officers. Around the cavalry

Fig. 7. Officers of the 17th Lancers at Lucknow, 1886. Lt. B.P. Portal is standing 4th from the left. He was then 19 and the 'new boy' in the regiment.

mess lay a suburb of roomy bungalows standing in their own walled grounds and gardens. Subalterns received a lodging allowance and shared the rent and the wages of servants to do their washing and cooking.

Just before dawn one was awakened by a dusky figure with a clammy hand and a razor. By 6 o'clock the regiment was on parade and we rode to a wide plain and drilled and manoeuvered for an hour and a half. We then returned to baths at the bungalow and breakfast at the mess. Then at nine, stables and orderly room till about half past ten. Then back to the bungalow before the sun attained its fiercest ray. We nipped across to luncheon at half past one and then returned to sleep till five o'clock. Now the station begins to live again. It is the hour of polo. It is the hour for which we have been living all day.

As the shadows lengthened, we ambled back, perspiring and exhausted to hot baths, rest and at 8.30 dinner, to the strains of the regimental band and the clinking of ice in well filled glasses. Then smoking in the moonlight till half past ten or eleven and 'so to bed'. Such was the long Indian day as I knew it for three years; and not such a bad day either.[3]

Bertram learned to play polo at Lucknow. He was in a team playing at Naini Tal, a hill station to the north east of Lucknow, in August 1887.[4] He also started a cricket eleven.[5]

GARRISON DUTIES IN ENGLAND AND EGYPT

By August 1889, Bertram was back at the regiment's home base at the Canterbury Cavalry depot.[6] From there the 17th Lancers took part in a review at Aldershot in the presence of Kaiser Wilhelm II of Germany who had acceded to the throne the previous year. Bertram went to the review with his colonel, Sir Drury Lowe, and had a ringside view. He wrote to his mother,

> There were about 13,000 men on each side… A start was made which was announced by a gun fired off directly the Emperor arrived. The cavalry of both sides quickly advanced and it was the prettiest thing of the whole day to see the first cavalry charge. Five regiments on one side and four on the other all galloping in line as hard as they could go and stopping about 20 yards apart. Then followed manoeuvres and a great deal of firing by artillery and infantry.
>
> The Emperor and his very large staff kept galloping about and seemed to be much interested. Just before the end of the fight the enemy's cavalry came charging up to make a sort of flank attack but there was a tremendous lot of firing and smoke and they received a most murderous fire from their own infantry! It was a pretty sight and I enjoyed it. It was awfully kind of Sir Drury to let me be with him. I should have seen very little otherwise.[7]

In October 1890 Bertram sailed with part of the regiment to Ismailia for garrison duty on the west bank of the Suez Canal. They were quartered at Abbasiyah near Cairo until October 1891. No letters from this period have been found but he no doubt enjoyed a relaxed life, similar to his time in India, since there were no hostilities while he was there.[8]

Fig. 8. 17th Lancers polo team at the Paris Tournament, 1893. Bertram is seated left.

The regiment came home and in June 1892 Bertram passed his examinations for promotion but it was not until 1895 that a vacancy appeared and he was made a Captain.[9] During this time the regiment was based at Hounslow, west of London, Preston in Lancashire, Shorncliffe near Folkestone, Leeds and then York.[10] This gave plenty of opportunities for polo, point-to-point races and shooting parties at the invitation of family friends.[11]

However, it was also a time of sadness and upheaval in the family. In 1892 Bertram's sister Eleanor lost her husband, Chaloner Chute, and she moved to Malshanger House with her four children. His cousin Melville Raymond died in 1893 followed by cousin Gerald in 1894. In the same year his sister Constance lost her husband, William Kingsmill. Bertram was close to all of them.

MADRAS

In March 1896, Bertram was appointed *aide de camp* to the newly arrived Governor of Madras, Sir Arthur Havelock.[12] It is not known how he came by this appointment but it would usually have been made through family connections. His rank and family background were suitable. This was a civil and not a military role but was normally carried out by junior officers on secondment from their regiments. For Bertram the advantage was that he would rub shoulders with important people who might help to advance his career. Maybe this was preferable to yet another spell of garrison duty. Maybe the title 'A.D.C. to the Governor of Madras' would, in due course, make him

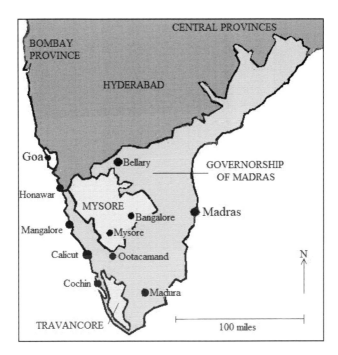

Map 2. The Governorship of Madras. Bertram visited all the places named on the map.

more marriageable. He arrived in Madras in March 1896.[13]

The Governor's area of responsibility in southern and eastern India was somewhat larger than England and significantly larger in population. It included five Princely States whose rulers enjoyed internal self-government, provided the British Political Resident approved. The largest of these were Mysore and Travancore.

The Princely States were ranked by the British in an order of precedence according to the number of guns to be fired in ceremonial salutes to the Maharajah. Mysore was one of three in India allowed a 21-gun salute whereas Travancore was only awarded 19 and Cochin 17.

The Governor was much engaged with civil administration but also had an important social role. In a world where etiquette and precedent were all important, the role of the A.D.C. was to ensure that his boss never put a foot wrong. There were receptions, dinner parties, balls and garden parties and Bertram seems to have thoroughly enjoyed it.

> Last night we had our big birthday ball here. It was a tremendous success and really lovely. We all took a great deal of trouble and were at it most of the day. There is no difficulty about tents in this country, the thing is to make them look pretty. We had about five large tents and covered the whole of the insides with hangings and pretty stuff with any amount of plants and greenery and all lit with Chinese lanterns. We had 350 people.[14]

He also had to introduce the guests to the Governor by name. Each one came carrying a card but Bertram found the very long Indian names difficult to pronounce and to get it wrong would have caused offence.

There was a steady stream of visitors to Government House, often the sons of the English aristocracy who were passing through. Part of Bertram's job was to look after them. One such was Winston Churchill, who was kicking his heels on garrison duty with his regiment at Bangalore.[15]

> We have got several people staying here at the moment including the young Winston Churchill. He is very amusing and a tremendous talker. He is now full of his experiences in the late frontier war and very interesting they are. He is extremely clever and rather self-opinionated but not disagreeably so. His book on the 'Malakand Field Force' has had a tremendous success and he has received any number of congratulatory messages including one from the Prince of Wales which he got here yesterday.[16]

The seat of government was at Guindy in the outskirts of Madras but in the hot season, from April to September, almost the whole administration moved to the hill station at Ootacamand known colloquially as 'Ooty'. At 7,000 feet above sea level it enjoyed a drier and cooler climate more to the liking of the British.

Bertram described his first journey to Ootacamand shortly after his arrival in Madras. It took four days, covering about 30 miles a day.

We left Madras on Friday afternoon. It was called a 'public' departure which meant that all European Madras had to congregate at the station to say 'goodbye'. We all travelled in tongas – a vehicle like a low 2-wheeled dog cart with a hood to it. They change ponies every five miles and go at a capital pace.

This house is delightful and the climate is ideal, 75deg in the daytime and I am quite glad of a blanket at night. I generally have a fire in the drawing room in the evening if I say it is necessary. Capt. Bingham is here and is Master of Fox Hounds. I am 1st whipper in. I have also been made secretary of the polo club. The first important duty here for all of us is to 'call' on everybody. It is an awful business but has to be done. The hours are from 12 till 2 and I go out every day.[17]

There being few foxes in India they hunted jackals instead. There was also big game hunting and on one occasion, Bertram shot a bison.[18] On another he was given a special licence to shoot a tusker elephant but, although he encountered many elephants, there were no tuskers to be seen which disappointed him greatly. Bertram enjoyed frequent polo matches including the Bangalore polo tournament when Government House raised a team.[19]

In May 1897 there was an important ten-day horse show at Ootacamand.

There were about 250 entries and all the best animals in their class in this part of India. The first class was for heavyweight hunters for which there were a lot of entries. I got 2nd prize, losing the first prize by just one mark. In the next class for lightweight-hunters I got 1st prize out of 28 entries. There were then lots more classes and on to the second day was the 'championship class' for which only horses which had won prizes could compete. This was a prize for the 'best horse in the show' and to my great delight I won it with my lightweight-hunter. The prize is a very handsome silver cup presented to the same horse I won a race with the other day.[20]

Fig. 9. Prize at a gymkhana

The following year Bertram came away with some more silverware.

Picnics in the woods were popular at Ooty but one of them did not go according to plan.

About 2 o'clock there was a sumptuous repast set out on the ground with every possible luxury. Everyone had just got their plates full when the first drops of rain came down followed by a perfect deluge. Pies, jellies, chickens and legs of mutton floated about in their dishes and everyone got drenched. We were about six miles from home so we knew if we did not eat we would not get another chance. It was one of the funniest sights I ever saw with 25 sane and rational human beings sitting wrapped up in Mackintoshes with umbrellas up tucking in to sodden food and trying to look cheerful.[21]

Every year the Governor went on tour around his patch for about two months. When possible they travelled by train or by sea in a luxurious 2,500 ton steamer. The next best option was to go by river in a steam launch or a cabin vessel manned by rowers. Going by road was the slowest. On one occasion, Bertram was carried for 18 miles on a track in the hills in a slung hammock which he found most uncomfortable.

The Governor made a point of visiting hospitals, jails, schools and public buildings which involved listening to very long speeches. Bertram was impressed with the schools, especially those run by Catholics, but wrote that 'educating the natives would make them think they were as good as the white man' and that this would lead to trouble. At one place a disturbance had been quelled by the British with the loss of 80 Indian lives. The Governor wanted to know how this had arisen and to put right any wrongs. This visit entailed some danger to His Excellency and his entourage travelled with loaded revolvers just in case. In the event his visit was very much welcomed.

There were visits to the Princely States of Mysore and Travancore with much ceremony involving decorated elephants, guards of honour and the obligatory gun salutes. At Mysore they were the guests of the Maharani Regent, the mother of the 13-year old Maharaja. Since the Maharani was 'a purdah lady', who was never to be seen in public, there were all kinds of problems of etiquette but the visit was judged to have been a great success.

These tours also gave opportunities for sight-seeing. Bertram particularly enjoyed visits to the old Portuguese city of Goa, Hindu temples and the waterfalls at Gairsuppa.

Back in Madras, the Governor had to deal with distress caused by famine in the north east of his area in 1897, though it did not affect southern India. He toured the affected area for a week.

> He was very well satisfied with all the arrangements for relief we have. As there is mercifully no famine down in the south of India he thinks the experience gained by those responsible for relief works may be very valuable when a famine does occur here. [22]

An outbreak of bubonic plague devastated Bombay Province in late 1896. Elaborate precautions were taken in the Madras Governorship for the isolation of suspected cases but in the event there were only two patients in Madras in 1897, one of whom had travelled from Poona. They both survived.

Bertram seems to have been enjoying this life and the duties were not arduous but it was definitely not soldiering. By the end of 1897 he was making enquiries about returning to his regiment. This was by no means automatic and depended on there being a vacancy. In April 1898, Bertram wrote to his brother Spencer.

> Our party moves today to Ootacamand. It is beginning to stoke up here now and we are glad to be going to cooler climes. I am quite

hoping to return to my regiment sometime this summer. If I can't get a vacancy I shall apply to come home on leave about November.[23]

It took another few months but eventually all was arranged and he arrived home two days before Christmas.[24]

CHAPTER 3

COURTSHIP AND MARRIAGE

Less than four months after returning home from Madras, Bertram married the Hon. Margaret Littleton on 12th April 1899.[1] He was 33. The story of their courtship illustrates the difficulties a young army officer could have in finding a wife.

At the age of 22, he was presented at court to the Prince of Wales at a levee held at St James' Palace in 1888.[2] This was the male equivalent of the presentation of debutantes. Presentation at Court was open to the landed gentry, the clergy, the professions and officers in the army and navy and but not generally to those only engaged in trade. Application was made to the Lord Chamberlain who checked that applicants were 'respectable'. Lists of those presented were published in the newspapers which identified young men who were marriageable in high society. They then attended fashionable social occasions during 'the season'.[3] As a Lieutenant, Bertram was not yet marriageable. He would have to get promotion before he could support a wife.

Garrison duty abroad meant almost exclusively male company and the chances of meeting a marriageable young lady were remote. Early marriage was seen as an impediment to a young officer's career and was made very difficult. A marriage allowance was not paid until an Indian Army officer was twenty-six, and it was necessary to seek the Colonel's permission to marry. This was often refused until a young officer had achieved the rank of Captain.[4]

In 1890 the Hon. Margaret Littleton was also presented at 'The Queen's Drawing Room' by her mother, the Lady Hatherton.[5] She was 21 and was always known as 'Mittie'. The Hatherton family wealth was based on landed estates at Penkridge in Staffordshire with mines, quarries and brick yards.[6] They lived at Teddesley Hall and also owned a London town house at 55 Warwick Square. The family came down for the London season.[7] Bertram's father also rented a town house at Eaton Square.[8]

Letters from the Blackwood family, who were mutual friends of the Portals and the Hathertons, show that Bertram and Mittie knew each other from childhood. Mittie's grandmother was the daughter of George Percy, 5th Duke of Northumberland. One of Bertram's early memories was going with his mother to Northumberland House, to see the Duchess of Northumberland in the court dress she had worn at one of Queen Victoria's afternoon 'Drawing Rooms'. He was impressed by the profusion of diamonds she wore.[9] Mittie was related to Henry Percy, Bertram's godfather and Mittie's great-grandmother was a Portal.

Having been presented at Court, Bertram was posted to Ismailia and remained there until November 1891.[10] There then followed a period of garrison duties in England. The signatures of Bertram and Spencer both appear at different times in Mittie's autograph book in 1893.[11] In November 1894 the Littleton family attended the Staffordshire County Infirmary Ball and amongst the party from Teddesley Hall was Mr B. Portal, 17th Lancers.[12] The following month the Portal family were at a ball at the Drill Hall in Basingstoke. Amongst their party was the Hon. Margaret Littleton.[13] Perhaps by then they were romantically entwined.

However, there is an undated letter from Bertram to Mittie, written from his sister Mary's house in Buckinghamshire, which makes it quite clear that Bertram had proposed to her and had been refused. He 'hoped that they might meet again some day and be the friends they had always been'. He then departed to Madras for three years and it seems likely that he took the job to be far away and to help him forget all about her. No letters between them from this period have come to light.

During this interval Mittie was becoming noticed for her fine singing voice and participation in amateur theatricals at house parties and charity events.[14] On his return to England from Madras, Bertram was invited, among 250 other guests, to a house party at Clandeboye House, the Irish residence of the Marquess of Dufferin and Ava. His eldest son, the Earl of Ava, had served with Bertram as a lieutenant in the 17th Lancers.[15] Mittie's father had been Military Secretary to the Marquess when he was Governor General of Canada. A programme of entertainment was organised on the tennis court.

> The Hon. Margaret Littleton sang in costume '*Just a little bit of string*' which proved most captivating and the demand for an encore was so persistent there was no denying it. The last item was a pantomime play, '*Bluebeard*'. The several characters were thoroughly expressed by Lord Plunkett (Bluebeard), Hon. Margaret Littleton (Fatima) and Capt. Portal was a creditable exponent of the long-expected brother.[16]

Bertram had revived his interest in acting from his schooldays. This was perhaps when Bertram renewed his proposal to Mittie since their engagement was announced in the press nine days later.[17] Bertram asked the Earl of Ava to be his best man.

The wedding on 12th April 1899 was dazzling. The whole village of Penkridge was decorated with flowers and there were three floral arches spanning the route from the church. Luncheon for 120 guests was provided in the dining room and morning room at Teddesley Hall. The officers of the 17th Lancers gave Bertram a silver salver inscribed with their names and the regimental motto.[18]

The smallest of the bridesmaids was Constance Portal, his brother Spencer's daughter, aged seven, who recalled the whole event.

*Fig. 10. Wedding day photograph of Bertram and
Mittie with the best man and bridesmaids.*

We travelled from Basingstoke in a Pullman rail car. It had two compartments. In the larger one sat my grandparents in armchairs and a big contingency of aunts and uncles and my mother. In the smaller compartment, on less grand chairs, sat part of the Malshanger household. Mr Sear, the butler, with whiskers high up on his cheeks, Mrs Giles, the cook, Lizzie the head housemaid, sundry ladies' maids and two footmen (young). I went next door and played 'snap' with one of the footmen.

At last we were at Teddesley, the hall all lights and Lady Hatherton's lovely welcoming smiling face and kisses. The next day was the wedding. Our hats were enormous and the bouquets were huge. The wedding was all right, I was used to being a bridesmaid. An elderly gentleman asked if he could have one of my roses. I said he couldn't, but he pulled one out, put it in his buttonhole and gave me a kiss. I was furious.[19]

Fig. 11. Bertram and Mittie, 1899.

At the time of the wedding there was a marriage settlement in which both families put assets into trust for the benefit of the couple and any children they might have.[20]

After the wedding the young couple went to live in Cork where the 17th Lancers were based. They took a house at Middle Glanmire Road in the city, about five miles from the barracks at Ballincollig. The house was large enough to accommodate four living-in servants.[21]

Little Constance Portal recalled them visiting Malshanger shortly after the wedding. 'Aunt Mittie's arrival was like sunshine and her fun just rippled. She broke all the rules.'[22]

CHAPTER 4

THE BOER WAR, 1900-1902

FIRST DEPLOYMENT TO SOUTH AFRICA,
February–June, 1900

At the start of the war in October 1899, the Boers in their two republics of Transvaal and the Orange Free State went on the offensive and besieged Ladysmith, Kimberley and Mafeking. The British seriously underestimated the capabilities of an irregular army of Boer farmers armed with the latest weapons. British attempts to relieve

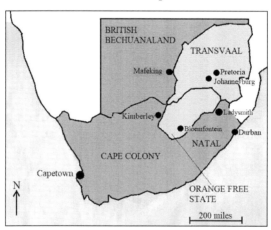

Map 3. Southern Africa in 1900.

the sieges were costly disasters. General Buller was relieved of his post and replaced by Lord Roberts, with General Kitchener as his second in command. They both arrived in December with reinforcements. Ladysmith and Kimberley were relieved in February 1900, and on 13th March the Boers surrendered Bloemfontein without a fight. Roberts waited there to reinforce and re-supply his armies before resuming the advance.

The 17th Lancers were summoned to South Africa in February 1900. This is the list of kit that Bertram had to assemble in addition to his uniforms.[1]

OFFICER'S KIT FOR SOUTH AFRICA

Colonial saddle complete with breastplate.	Field cap,1 shirt, 1 pr socks.
Wallets.	1 pr drawers, night cap, towel.
Sword in khaki cover.	Knife/fork/spoon combined.
Shoe case with 1 fore, 1 hind shoe and nails.	Small tin of Vaseline.
Leather saddle bag.	Cholera belt.
Cavalry canteen in khaki cover.	Leather cup.
Nose bag.	Comb, razor, shaving brush,
Poncho on rear of saddle.	Hairbrush, toothbrush, soap.
Colonial bridle with headrope.	1 pr scissors.
Emergency rations.	Housewife (thread, buttons and
Telescope, map, wire clippers.	needle).
Blanket under saddle.	Spare pipe. Handkerchief.

Fig. 12. Bertram's spare horse carrying his kit and its own forage.

Bertram would have a second horse to carry all this kit. A cholera belt was a flat strip of red flannel or knitted wool about six feet long and six inches wide which was twisted around the abdomen under a shirt. It was believed to protect the wearer from cholera.

Mittie was then six months pregnant and would have known from the newspapers what the risks to her husband were. The Boer farmers had already shown that they could inflict heavy casualties on the British. Bertram's best man at their wedding had been killed during the siege of Ladysmith in January.[2] As well as battle casualties, the newspapers also reported the even greater numbers of deaths from typhoid fever and dysentery.[3] The army paid little attention to hygiene or the state of their field hospitals.[4]

The regiment was divided into four squadrons each commanded by a major. Bertram wrote in his diary that he was disappointed not to have a squadron but reckoned he was 'next in line' for promotion.[5]

Their ship, the *Victorian*, left Tilbury docks in a snowstorm.[6] Because of strong winds she had to heave-to off North Foreland until the pilot

Fig. 13. The regiment parading in the snow just prior to their departure for South Africa, February 1900.

could be landed. A gale ensued and the heavy rolling affected their horses very badly. Nine of them died.

On the 23rd February they arrived at Las Palmas in the Canary Islands where they received news that Kimberley had been relieved and that a large column was advancing on Bloemfontein. Bertram was inoculated against typhoid fever but his servant and some of the officers and men refused it. He thought it should have been compulsory and not left to 'stupid boys of 19'.[7] The voyage was otherwise pleasant and uneventful though another 23 horses died.[8]

On arrival in Capetown on 10th March they heard that the siege of Ladysmith had been lifted. There was 'tremendous cheering' but Bertram recorded that their 'chief fear now is that the war may be over before we get there'. It is understandable. Bertram had been in the army for 16 years but had never seen action. This was his chance to excel and to receive medals, honours and promotion.

They marched to Maitland camp, about four miles from Capetown

Fig.14. Capt. B. P. Portal outside his tent at Bloemfontein.

where their principal task was to get their horses fit for action. Bertram was sent off to buy 16 pack ponies and five chargers for the officers. There was plenty of opportunity to visit the Mount Nelson Hotel in Capetown where Bertram met Rudyard Kipling, 'a very undistinguished little man'.[9] He also met Winston Churchill, then a newspaper reporter, who was very frustrated because he could not get a permit to go to Bloemfontein.[10]

It was not until 4th April that the regiment left Capetown by rail for Bloemfontein, a 600-mile journey that took four days with regular stops to feed the horses. They camped about two miles north of the town where they learned that the 17th Lancers were to be part of the 3rd Cavalry Brigade under the command of General Gordon.

Whilst they were waiting, two of Bertram's friends in other regiments died of typhoid fever and he attended their funerals. Finally, on 23rd April, the advance to the north began. There was great excitement in the camp.

From then on, Bertram wrote his diary as if he were compiling a military report of manoeuvres, engagements, advances and retreats. He did not say what he felt about the casualties, except for a single comment, 'How horrible this war is and all my best friends are being killed'. He did not write about the privations they suffered though he did complain in his letters to Mittie about how cold he was at night. They travelled without their tents and bivouacked in the open to match the mobility of the Boers. Much of the time they were on half-rations

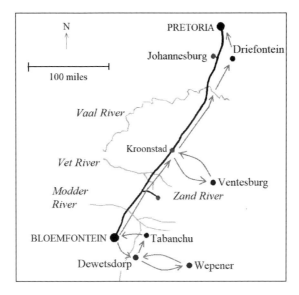

Map 4. Movements of the 17th Lancers, April-June 1900. The distance from Bloemfontein to Pretoria by the railway line shown on the map is 280 miles.

because their supply wagons could not keep up with them. There was never any bread and they had to make do with hard biscuit. Sometimes their water supplies were frozen in the morning. The waterproofs and blankets supplied by the army were useless. Bertram wrote home with a request for 400 sweaters for the men of his regiment which were sent but they never arrived.[11] Mittie and various children at Malshanger all knitted scarves and Balaclavas for them too.[12]

The first task for the 3rd Cavalry Brigade was to attack Boer forces to the south east of Bloemfontein. They had taken Dewetsdorp and were besieging the garrison at Wepener.[13] There was a danger that the Boers might retake Bloemfontein after the main army had advanced to the north. As the 17th Lancers reached the Modder River they came under fire but the Boers retreated as they continued to advance. Bertram did not reveal in his diary what it was like to be under fire for the first time but he did in his letters to Mittie. A man whose horse had been killed under him was running away from the enemy on foot. One of Bertram's troopers got the man up behind him on his horse but he fell off, exhausted.

I jumped down and put him on my horse with myself behind him. It was very exciting as we were well within range and bullets were whizzing past us but we got out of it all right.

I really am thoroughly enjoying it and pleased to find that bullets are not as alarming as I thought they would be.[14]

When they crossed the river and climbed the steep hill on the other side the Boers retreated without taking advantage of the situation. The 17th Lancers chased them out of Dewetsdorp, relieved Wepener and then pushed them towards Tabanchu. Here they came under heavy fire from three sides and had to retreat. Other forces worked round to encircle the Boers who then retired northwards. Bloemfontein and the main line of communication was now secure and they were ordered back there. It had taken 13 days and it cost them 150 horses. Bertram wrote that 'Double work, double loads and half food has been the mischief'. He went to the remount depot to get more horses but they were still unfit from their journey from Capetown.

After only two days rest the 17th Lancers were ordered to catch up with the main army which had already left in two columns, advancing on either side of the railway line. The British now had a huge numerical advantage and Boer policy was not to risk a pitched battle but to fight rearguard actions where they could inflict casualties and then retreat to fight another day.

The bridges across the Vet and Zand rivers had been blown up by the enemy. They crossed the Vet unopposed and crossed the Zand after a brief artillery duel. They were fortunate. The main army ahead of them had encountered fierce Boer resistance at the Zand crossing resulting in many casualties.[15] They caught up with the main army about eight miles from Kroonstad where they came under artillery fire with shells whizzing just over their heads, exploding 100 yards behind them. Since it was late in the day they paused and then bivouacked. In the morning the Boers had gone. The 17th Lancers were the first troops into Kroonstad the next day. At this point Bertram was promoted to major and took command of C Squadron with 94 cavalrymen.[16]

After two days' rest, word came that there were about 500 Boers at Ventesberg and the 17th Lancers were ordered west to chase them off. The rumour proved to be false and they were ordered back again. When the advance was resumed, the 17th Lancers formed the rearguard. The Vaal River was crossed unopposed and they eventually reached Driefontein, about 5 miles east of Johannesburg. They were very short of food. By this time Johannesburg had fallen unopposed and the gold mines were in British hands. The Boers attempted to ambush the 3rd Cavalry in their camp at Dreifontein but their outposts were alert and the Boers were driven off.

Intelligence was then received that Pretoria was being evacuated by the enemy and the 3rd Cavalry was ordered to advance there as fast as possible. Off they went with their best horses but they were diverted to cut a railway line and one of the Guards Regiments arrived there first. The capitals of both Boer republics were now in British hands and it was generally assumed that the war was over.

The next day, June 7th, Bertram received a telegram which read, 'Boy, both well'. Mittie had given birth.[17] Bertram wrote back about what names he should have and, once this was decided, that he must be put down for Eton.[18] This was joyful news but the next morning he began to have pain in his right knee which surprised him because he

Fig. 15. Telegram, 7th June 1900.

had not injured it in any way. It became so severe that he had to go to the doctor who sent him to Bourke's Hospital. This depressed him badly because he had to hand over his squadron to someone else. He found the hospital, 'nice and comfortable and the nurses are all Boer young ladies who were kind and attentive. The luxury of a bed is indescribable'. However, the knee swelled up and he needed morphia for the pain. The doctors decided to operate, which they did without anaesthetic, but it produced no improvement. A second operation two days later was performed under chloroform.

A few days later he wrote to Mittie,

> I started the day by having another cut in my poor leg. This is the 4th occasion that the medical authorities have seen fit to make an incision into my innocent limb and I sincerely hope it will be the last.
>
> I only wish to heaven this whole thing was over. All I want is to get home to my wife and family. This is not my idea of matrimony at all. I have been lying on my back now for 17 days and I am so sick of it.[19]

He was fortunate that the surgeons did not do his knee any lasting harm for that could have meant the end of his military career. It was then decided to send him back to England and he was allocated a trooper, Barnard, as his 'body servant' for the whole journey. He was carried on to the train along with about 90 other invalids and several nurses. They had to wait at Kroonstad for another train going north which they heard later had been blown up by the Boers with heavy casualties. (This was a warning of things to come. The Boers had lost their capital cities but their armies had not been defeated.) The journey was otherwise uneventful but it took a week to get to Capetown and Wynburg Hospital. He found it very comfortable and he was cheered by many visitors. With the passage of time his knee improved.

Bertram boarded the *Assaye* on 21st August along with his servant Barnard and 1,400 other invalids but he had a 2-berth cabin to himself. It was a 'wonderful and pleasant voyage' and as the knee improved he was allowed to bear weight on his right leg.

When the ship docked at Southampton on 10th September his two brothers were there to meet him. On arrival at Malshanger he found Mittie and their son, then over three months old.[20] He described it as the happiest day of his life. He was given a hero's welcome and Bertram told the assembled company that the voyage 'had done him a world of good and that the lameness is better already'.[21]

Bertram, Mittie and little Melville then returned to their house in Cork.[22] Since his knee was no longer a problem it must have been a relaxing break but the war was continuing and his recall to South Africa would only be a matter of time.

SECOND DEPLOYMENT TO SOUTH AFRICA,
August 1901-September 1902

After the fall of Pretoria in June 1900, Lord Roberts offered amnesty to Boers who would return to their farms and many did so. However, there was a small group of diehard leaders determined to pursue a guerrilla war in Cape Colony where they hoped to recruit the Boers living there.

Part of the British response was to set up blockhouses and wire fences, partitioning off the entire conquered territory in the Orange Free State and Transvaal. If farmers were not at home when a British

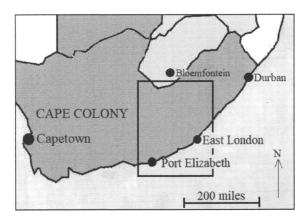

Map 5. 17th Lancers' area of operations, Eastern Cape Colony, September 1901-May 1902.

patrol arrived it was assumed they were away with the 'rebels'. Their farmhouses, crops and livestock were destroyed and families were moved into 'concentration camps', a policy fiercely criticised in Parliament and the British press. The Boers, although they had the occasional success, were being steadily weakened by British mobile columns.

Bertram served in the Eastern Cape for eight months until the end of the war and then had a long wait for repatriation. Once again, he wrote a daily diary.[23] The task for the cavalry was to defeat several Boer 'commandos' roaming there, each of about 80 men.

The area of operations is indicated by the British supply bases marked on the map lying south of the Orange River which formed the border with the Orange Free State. The country lies at the southern end of the Drakensberg mountain range.

Bertram embarked on the *Templemore* on 16th August 1901. He found that he was the senior officer on the ship and was put in command of all the troops on board. He made it his business to give the best possible care to the horses on board and kept the men busy with this task for five hours a day. They lost 19 horses but Bertram thought that a casualty rate of less than five per cent was very creditable.

On arrival at Capetown he was ordered to stay on board till the ship reached Port Elizabeth and, after much delay, he finally rejoined his regiment at Stormberg on 14th September where he met up with his old friends. Three days later he went by train to Tarkastad only to hear that Major Sandeman's squadron had been 'practically wiped out' at Moddersfontein west of the town in a Boer attack the day before. He rode out there.

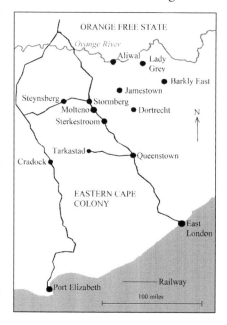

Map 6. Detail of Map 5.

The most dreadful sight I ever saw. All the ground littered with dead horses, broken rifles, smoldering wagons and the bodies of three officers and 30 men laid out ready for burial. Sandeman and Vivian were wounded. Sheridan, Morritt and Russell killed.

The attack took place at 12 noon just as men and horses were feeding but all ordinary precautions had been taken. Patrols had been sent out in the morning but it was misty and it was difficult for them to see any distance. An observation post was out at the time of the attack but the Boers crept all along a deep watercourse on foot. A frontal attack was made by the enemy and when the squadron met this attack all the men in the watercourse took up a position to the rear of the squadron so that our poor fellows found themselves being fired on from front and rear and they were practically surrounded. The Boers were all dressed in our khaki uniforms and they were thought to be some of our own men till they opened fire at quite short range. Morritt with his troop was about 20 yards from the enemy and shouted 'fix bayonets, charge' when he was shot with an explosive bullet and half his head was blown off. Sheridan was shot through the throat when about 10 yards from the enemy. If it was the most daring attack it was certainly the most gallant defence of the war. There was no thought of any white flag – they fought and died like men. There were over 70 casualties in a fighting strength of not more than 130 and about 50% of the casualties were killed which is an enormous proportion and due chiefly to the soft-nosed cartridges which were used by the enemy. Several of these have been picked up. These bullets inflict most ghastly wounds. They took everything from the pockets of the dead. Not even letters were left.[24]

A clergyman from Tarkastad came out for the funeral. A long trench had been dug and the 33 bodies were laid side by side A small wooden cross was put up at the end where the officers were buried.

A few days later Bertram received a copy of a telegram from Gen. French to Col. Haig to tell the column commanders that it was 'his distinct order to try by summary court martial and shoot on the spot any prisoners attempting to imitate British uniforms'. The 17th Lancers had a score to settle with the Boers. Ten days later Bertram's squadron took a prisoner in a British uniform. As he was being marched to the place of execution he made a run for it towards a little wood. The soldiers shot him dead before he got there.

The 17th Lancers never operated as a single regiment. Their four squadrons, each of about 130 men, were attached to several columns under different colonels. Bertram's squadron worked alongside elements of other British regiments, locally raised troops of lesser quality and a few field guns.

Despite what had happened at Moddersfontein, some senior officers were complacent. One day, Bertram found his column winding up a narrow gorge with dense thorn bush on either side. He pointed out to his colonel that this would be a perfect site for an ambush. The colonel replied, 'Yes, but these fellows never stay for us. They always belt directly they see us'. Shortly afterwards a fusillade rang out and it was clear they were in a very dangerous position. The colonel said, 'Portal, I think you had better retire your men.' This was easier said than done since the column was spread out along the narrow path. Bertram rallied some troops and managed to get to higher ground to cover the retreat and the column escaped with the loss of a few horses and four men wounded. Bertram observed that if the Boers had been there in force the whole column would have been annihilated. The next day they negotiated the gorge 'in the proper way' with men on the tops on either side. The Boers had long since gone.

The whole British operation depended on the rail links with Port Elizabeth and East London. On his way up by train Bertram had noted blockhouses every mile and wire between them to protect the line and bridges from Boer attacks. Each blockhouse was manned by eight soldiers and they were connected by telegraph. It was hoped this would prevent the Boers moving from one side of the track to the other but it proved to be ineffective.

The British columns in the area needed bases away from the railway which were supplied by convoys of ox wagons each drawn by 16 oxen. A convoy might consist of 70 or more wagons and was heavily guarded as it moved at a stately pace of not more than two miles an hour.

To match the speed of the Boers a column often travelled light, with food and forage for their horses for just three days. Without tents, they bivouacked in the open in all weathers and the nights were very cold. The other disadvantage was that they had to return to one of their bases every third day. To

Fig. 16. British blockhouse.

increase their endurance they used pack mules to carry stores but they were slower and sometimes could not catch up with them. On several occasions they and their horses were without food for over 24 hours.

By this time the Boer commandos were greatly outnumbered and their strategy was to harass the British whenever they could but to avoid major battles by keeping constantly on the move. They knew the country well whereas the British relied on maps that were often out of date and local guides who were not always reliable.

By using several columns the British could cover more ground in their search for the Boers but communication between the columns was a constant problem. Whenever possible they used a heliograph. This was a device with a mirror using the rays of the sun to send messages in Morse code over 20 miles or more. It did not work on cloudy days. Carrier pigeons were also used but scouts and messengers on horseback were their mainstay. That meant that by the time messages were received and acted on the Boers had usually gone elsewhere. Messengers were also vulnerable to capture by the Boers. Bertram recorded that on one occasion, a courier was sent back with a message from the Boer commander which read, 'If you khakis want to catch us you will have to gallop a lot faster than that!' One tactic was to march by night in the hope of surprising the Boers at dawn. The trouble was that, by the time they arrived, their horses were tired out and the Boers galloped away on their fresh mounts. Such were the difficulties the British faced.

For seven months, Bertram's squadron crisscrossed the area riding up to 30 miles a day and often by night with very little rest. They never encountered an entire Boer commando and engaged small parties of them on seven occasions only. They killed or wounded a few, took prisoners, horses, saddles, rifles and ammunition. On three occasions the Boers did the same to them. Only once was there the opportunity for a cavalry charge which is what they had all trained for.

> At about 3pm the Boers were sighted by our advanced patrols on a perfectly level plain. The hills were about eight miles off and we could see a straggling party of Boers about four miles off. Col. Munro gave the order to gallop and away we went. It was the most exciting thing I have ever done. Our horses were fairly fit and all the men mad with excitement. We gained on them steadily but as we got on the ground became more uneven and we kept losing sight of the enemy and had to keep going to the tops of ridges to see which way they had gone. This of course made us lose time and finally we got to the hills and found they had arrived first and had gone up a steep and narrow kloof to Roode Nek.[25] Col. Munro settled to push on up the kloof and when we had got about two thirds of the way up the Boers opened rather a heavy fire from the top of the hill, range about 1500 yards. We blazed back but the enemy were quite hidden and we could only shoot where we supposed them to be. Three men of our column were slightly wounded and 10 of our horses shot. As far as we were concerned the only result was one Boer prisoner. It was very bad luck not to be able to get into them and, I think, well worth the attempt. With just a little longer distance on the flat or if they had had a little less start we certainly should have caught a good many.[26]

On another occasion Bertram's squadron was ordered to do a night march which turned out to include a mountain road with a cliff on one side and a precipice on the other with no fence. It became so dangerous that he had to call a halt until it was light. They arrived at their destination safely but the next day the orders were to return the way they had come. It was all very disheartening. In October, Bertram wrote,

> As far as we can see there is no reason why this warfare should not go on another year or more. If the country was loyal their existence would be impossible but as it is almost entirely disloyal they get help from everywhere and live fairly comfortably.

In fact, the Boer farmers living in Cape Colony were divided in their loyalties. Later on, he encountered several who gave information to the British about the whereabouts of the commandos. He was told that they were short of food, ammunition, horseshoes, boots and clothes.

At Christmas 1901 Bertram distributed the Christmas presents sent by his parents to the squadron. He had probably organized it himself. Each man got a cardboard box containing a pipe, a pound of tobacco, a pair of socks and six red and white handkerchiefs suitable for nose, neck or hat. The men were quite delighted. The squadron also received a Christmas present from their commanders.

> Col. Munro has sent a very complimentary telegram to Col. Haig about my squadron which has pleased Col. Haig very much and he has published the telegram in regimental orders with some supplementary remarks by himself as to how proud he is to command such a regiment. As a matter of fact, the squadron has never had the chance of distinguishing itself in any way so the praise is really not merited.

Bertram was being too modest about their achievements. The result of their exertions was that the Boers were wholly on the defensive and were gaining no military or political advantage. The Boer population of Cape Colony did not rise up in their support. Their only chance of success would have been to blow up the railway bridges or attack the ox convoys on which the whole British effort depended. It was a tactic they had employed in the first phase of the war but now they did not have the military strength to achieve it.

As time went on the generals became frustrated by the lack of success of Bertram's column. The commanders took their orders from General French who was instructed in turn by Lord Roberts and Lord Kitchener. In his diary, Bertram spared nothing in his criticism of all of them. General French had previously let them know that he was pleased by their efforts but at the end of January he twice said how disappointed he was with them. It was not the best way to maintain morale. In February Bertram's colonel received a message from General French by telegram telling him that he was being judged by results and that he was to take three months' leave. That should never have been done by telegram and everyone in the camp was furious. Bertram confided to his diary that Colonel Munro had carried out his orders from above with great energy and it was not his fault if there were almost no Boers in the area to be caught. However, the result was that Major Portal was given the command of a column which would normally have fallen to a colonel.

This was in effect a promotion but it left Bertram with a problem. Back in December a group of married officers had been discussing how they could get their wives out to South Africa since the war seemed to be dragging on without end. Bertram had written to his brother Spencer,

This job we are on is quite a new experience for all of us because we are quite cut off from the world, are miles from any railway and we hear absolutely nothing about what is going on elsewhere. Progress seems mighty slow. It seems to me that what is wanted is troops to hold places after Boers have been driven out of a certain district. What so often happens is that when we have cleared one, we are then moved to clear another. Brother Boer then quietly treks back to the district where he originally was.

I am awfully fit and never feel my knee a bit. I often wish it would be possible for you to come and spend a couple of weeks with us in camp. You would love it. You could share my tent and come out with us on trek. I wish you would take two months leave and do it.

You know Douglas Haig is our Colonel now. He was asking after you the other day. He is an awfully nice fellow and one of the up and coming Wellingtons. He will be a big swell one of these days.

I want Mittie to come out here in the spring, about March. She is longing to come and it would be a good chance to see the country. If we are then as busy as we are now it would be no use her staying but she would enjoy the trip and I could probably get 10 days leave to be with her in Capetown.[27]

Neither of his wishes about family visits seems very sensible. Bertram's diary reveals his constant and intense frustration about the delays in getting mail and parcels from home. Separation from his wife and family were clearly affecting him badly. In response to his letter to Spencer he received a telegram from Mittie to say that he must ask the authorities for an 'indulgence passage'. This meant a passage on a troop ship at the army's expense. On 6th January Bertram received the message that 'The Chief cannot sanction indulgence passage for wife of Major Portal as he does not wish officers who are actively employed to bring wives out.' Bertram's response to Mittie was 'Indulgence passage refused. Come without'. She replied, 'Sailing *Kildonan Castle* Feb. 8th.' She was coming at family expense leaving Melville, who was then 21 months old, with the family and Nan Jagg. Mittie would soon be in Capetown but there was no prospect of him getting leave and it was expressly contrary to the orders of the Commander in Chief himself.

Bertram duly got his command and was once again crisscrossing the country out of contact for most of the time. Mittie arrived on 27th February with no word from him. She booked a room at the Mount Nelson Hotel along with other wives she had met on the boat. It was the best hotel in Capetown.

A few days later she heard that General French could not possibly allow leave and that Lord Roberts had banned officers' wives from leaving Capetown. She felt depressed and wished she had not come. Nevertheless, she was pleasantly occupied with swimming, walking, riding and sightseeing, visits to the races and dining with new friends.[28]

She had to kick her heels in this way for six weeks and then on 12th April, their wedding anniversary, Bertram suddenly got a message that three weeks' leave was granted from the same evening. It seems likely that someone was 'pulling strings' for him, probably Douglas Haig. When Bertram arrived at the station, Mittie thought,

> He was looking well and quite smart in a new khaki coat, not the worn-out warrior I had expected. However, the first thing he did was to buy a new cap and new boots. We drove straight up to Mount Nelson and his servant Newman followed with the baggage. Then he had a wash and shave and we had an excellent breakfast.[29]

They then had three glorious weeks together before Bertram had to return to his military duties on 8th May. By then it was well known that peace negotiations were well advanced and chasing the Boers was pursued with less vigour than before. As one of Bertram's soldiers remarked, 'You wouldn't want to get shot at this stage of the war'. The peace agreement was signed on 31st May but Bertram's column did not get the news for another five days.

Mittie found it difficult to get a berth to go home but finally left on 3rd June. On the same day Bertram received a message from Colonel Haig to select a group of 11 men to represent the regiment at the King's coronation. The plan was to embark them from Capetown forthwith but it never happened. The King became dangerously ill and the coronation was postponed. Bertram then had to trek with his squadron all the way to Capetown, a distance of over 500 miles. His diary ends on 29th June when they still had 200 miles to go. They did not leave until 28th September when the *German* left Capetown for England with Colonel D. Haig, Major B.P. Portal and 527 men of 17th Lancers on board.[30]

In July 1902 Lord Kitchener issued his final report on the war and mentioned Major Portal in his dispatch, though he did not say why.[31] He was almost certainly recommended by Douglas Haig. Officers of his rank were usually mentioned for their leadership qualities rather than conspicuous bravery. In eight months of hard service, Bertram had only seen action in seven brief encounters with small enemy forces and had rarely been in any danger. To be mentioned in dispatches was very important for Bertram's career. It opened the way for honours and promotion and without it he was going nowhere as the army would contract after the war.

In November it was announced that he was to be awarded the Distinguished Service Order which he received from the king in December. His rank was duly augmented to 'Brevet Major'. This was an army device to acknowledge outstanding service without a corresponding increase in pay but it paved the way to further promotion.

CHAPTER 5

COLONEL OF THE REGIMENT, 1902-1907

EDINBURGH, October 1902-September 1905

When the 17th Lancers arrived in England they were sent straight to Edinburgh where the regiment was split up. Col. Haig and his contingent went on to Glasgow whilst Major Portal, as his second in command, remained in Edinburgh with his contingent at Piershill Barracks.[1] There was ample scope for training men and horses, with a good covered riding school, an equitation field and, above all, a splendid expanse of sand at Portobello beach, less than a mile from the barracks.[2]

Life was good for the Portal family in Edinburgh. They lived in a comfortable house in Bellfield Road with Portobello beach at the end of the street looking out to the Firth of Forth.[3] The cavalrymen exercised their horses there every morning and the barracks was a short walk from their house. Two daughters, Charlotte and Hyacinthe (always known as Hytie), were born while they were there. Bertram was promoted to Lieutenant Colonel and commander of the regiment when Douglas Haig became Inspector of Cavalry in India.[4] The only sadness was that Bertram's mother died in November 1903.[5]

He would have been busy. The reserve regiment from the Curragh in Ireland joined them and there were new recruits to be trained.[6] The regiment had to be physically fit and effective and this was tested at exercises in the Cairngorm mountains. A northern 'blue' force moving from Blair Athol was to raid the arsenal and stores at Dunkeld, 21 miles to the south east. The southern 'red' force, under Lt. Col. Portal, was to defend Dunkeld, pending the arrival of reinforcements.[7] A newspaper reporter embedded with the attackers recorded,

> Up to now the honours have rested with the defending force. Col. Portal has distributed his troops with admirable skill, blocking every route and baiting every road with clever traps. The troops under Portal are displaying trickery, finesse and skill in concealment that command our unwilling admiration.
>
> Punctually at midnight on Sunday our troops set out when news arrived that the enemy had discovered our plan of attack so at the last minute it had to be completely altered. Our march had scarcely begun when a thick Scottish mist fell, later changing to a heavy downpour. Soon every man was soaked. At each mile travelled the land became more boggy, horses floundered and there was no shelter.
>
> This afternoon, quitting our own lines, I rode down to the enemy positions. I found admirably placed positions, scouts everywhere supported in the rear by an easily mobile main body.[8]

During the night, the northern force was able to capture half a squadron of the defenders and seize a position overlooking their camp. The judges thought they did not have enough men there to do significant harm so Bertram's reputation remained intact. 'Hostilities' then ceased, the men having been out for 36 hours without tents, blankets or change of clothing in heavy rain.[9]

The regiment was inspected by Field Marshal Lord Roberts in August 1903 and he appeared well pleased.[10] A year later they were inspected by Major General Robert Baden Powell of Mafeking fame.[11] About 5,000 people came to watch and take photographs of him. The Lancers demonstrated shooting from the saddle at full gallop, bare back riding and clearing hurdles with arms folded. Later, the officers shot at targets

Fig. 17. 17th Lancer's polo team at the Hurlingham Club. B.P. Portal is on the right.

in the sea with their revolvers and the general seemed well satisfied.[12] The following year, Baden Powell wrote to Bertram for advice on cavalry training which he duly gave.[13]

There seemed to be plenty of time for Bertram to indulge his passion for polo. He captained the 17th Lancers team who triumphed in the inter-regimental competition, beating the 8th Hussars in the final in 1903 at the Hurlingham Club in London.[14] To do that he needed to keep several polo ponies and often bought and sold ponies to ensure he had the very best.[15]

Life was also very sociable. Bertram went fox-hunting with the Borders Hunt and helped to organise their point-to-point races.[16] He also went to shoot with the Duke of Buccleuch and the Duke of Northumberland. On another occasion with Lord Alverstoke at Dunmaglass, seven guns dispatched 732 brace of grouse, 47 hares and four stags in the course of a week.[17]

The highlight of their stay in Edinburgh was the state visit of the King and Queen when the 17th Lancers provided the guard of honour.

Bertram was invited to a royal dinner party at Dalkeith Palace amongst only 17 distinguished guests.[18] He also lunched with the Duke of Connaught, dined with the High Commissioner for Scotland at Holyrood Palace and with the High Constables at the City Chambers at the Balmoral Hotel.[19] The regimental band played in the parks at week-ends and for many social occasions which was popular with the locals.[20] In July 1905 there was a torchlight revue at Piershill Barracks when the parade ground was lit by limelight for displays of horsemanship.[21]

Fig. 18. Bertram in 1904.

By July 1905 it was known that the regiment would be going to India. This must have caused Mittie and Bertram much heartache because the children would be left behind. Melville was five, Charlotte was not yet two and Hytie was seven months old. Mittie had to go because the British army expected that a colonel's wife would act as an unpaid 'social worker' for the wives of the married men in the regiment. India was still not considered a healthy place for very young children because of the climate and many endemic diseases, especially malaria, typhoid fever, plague and cholera. Bertram's father was 83 and unwell and they might not see him again.

Preparations were made and Bertram sold his polo ponies.[22] On September 4th, Mittie was amongst the advance party to leave that evening, including 49 women, 43 children and 100 soldiers.[23] Hundreds turned out to see them off and it took 40 policemen to keep the road clear for them. When the main body of the regiment left the next evening an estimated 10,000 people were at the station to say farewell with 'much cheering and singing'.[24] Their troopship, the *Assaye,* left Southampton on 7th September for Bombay.[25] When they arrived three weeks later, Bertram received the news that his father had died unexpectedly ten days after they left.

Bertram's uncle Melville had died the previous year. It would have been expected that one of his sons would inherit the family estates. However, his two older sons had pre-deceased him and the third son, Alaric, had a nervous condition and was unfit to manage any business. Uncle Robert had died in 1888 leaving only a daughter. It had been known for some years that the estates would pass to Bertram's elder brother William who moved to Laverstoke House from Southington House near Overton village. William had already taken over the running of the paper mill in his father's declining years.[26]

MEERUT, 1905-1907

Meerut is a town about 30 miles north east of Delhi. The British built a large barracks there in the early 19th century. It was at Meerut in 1857 that the Indian Mutiny started when sepoys attacked and killed their British officers. The military cantonment was a town in itself, accommodating four batteries of field artillery and four British regiments as well as Indian regiments with British officers.[27]

Mittie's first task was to get settled into their bungalow which came with a small army of house servants and gardeners, none of whom spoke English. When she realized the limitations of communication by sign-language she resolved to learn Hindustani which Bertram already spoke quite well.[28]

The 17th Lancers consisted of 18 officers and 483 other ranks.[29] The problem for a regimental garrison commander in India was how to keep 500 high-spirited young men out of trouble when there was no war to fight. Trouble meant admissions to hospital with typhoid fever, alcoholism or venereal disease and court cases which generally resulted from the mistreatment of Indians. To Bertram, success meant that 'the men are happy and contented, there is the minimum of crime and a maximum of soldiering and athletics'.[30] He wrote in the regimental magazine, the *White Lancer*,

> The cleverest soldier in the world is no use unless he is thoroughly fit for war and the only way to keep in training is going in vigorously for games and sports and at the same time leading a careful and steady life. In the 17th Lancers it has always been so and there is no doubt that this is the main reason why the number of men in hospital has kept so low in the recent hot weather.[31]

He was fortunate that the regimental medical officer sent out with them had instructions to promote inoculation for typhoid fever which was still not compulsory. In the year they arrived, 108 men at Meerut were admitted to hospital with typhoid and 22 of them died. Two years later admissions were down to 18 and only 4 died.[32]

Bertram organized sports competitions and football matches for the men and there were the usual manoeuvres, exercises and camps.

He enjoyed his big game hunting.

> Lately Major Smyth has been out again in Berar, his companions being two officers of the 17th Lancers, Capt. Alan Fletcher and Col. Portal. The latter only remained with the party a short time but got a panther. Major Smyth and Capt. Fletcher had a great shoot. Before returning they accounted for 33 game – not including the small game – including four tigers and six panthers, besides sambur and cheetah stags.[33]

This activity was encouraged by the army. It was good for public relations because these dangerous animals threatened Indian villages. It also encouraged good marksmanship as it was best to kill or bring down the animal at the first shot. A lightly wounded tiger was extremely hazardous.

Bertram and Mittie joined hunts for jackals with dogs and Bertram also loved hunting boars on horseback with spears. Pig-sticking was the most popular sport at Meerut. The season started in November with competitive meets every two weeks and continued till the rains came in June.[34] Mittie described the scene.

> Our camp is delightful under some trees. Mrs Coote brought her cook and provisions for two or three days and we each brought a bearer, a water man and syces (grooms) for the horses. Every morning we get up in the dark at 5.30 as the sun begins to rise, riding to the line of elephants and beaters. Then begins the slow march through what is called jungle but what I would call prairie. A pig gets up and away with four men after it. They constantly lose it and sometimes the men get bad falls. The one who gets his spear in first wins the heat and they leave off. If the pig is badly hurt they finish it off. I was glad when Bertram was out of it.[35]

She sent Melville a helpful explanation.

> Dads has gone away for a few days to hunt wild pig. He gallops after them and spears them which is very dangerous. The pig has long tusks and if a man falls off his horse the pig rushes at him and then eats him.[36]

Fig. 19. Bertram's stud at Meerut.

Bertram took his polo seriously and played for the regimental polo team. He had a stud of ten horses, including his polo ponies. A good polo pony could cost £55 and he had to pay for their forage and transport to tournaments at other stations as well as the syces to look after them. However, the 17th were defeated by the 9th Lancers in March 1906 'because their ponies were too slow'.[37] At the inter-regimental polo tournament held at Meerut the following month they were defeated in the first round by four goals to two.[38]

In December 1905 the Prince of Wales, later George V, toured British India and Burma and Bertram was presented. He wrote to Melville,

> I drove out one evening and went to a beautiful great tent with carpets and curtains and pictures on the walls. It was not cold because there was a fireplace with a good fire burning. At the head of the room stood the Prince of Wales. When I came near an officer shouted out, 'Colonel Portal'. I made a low bow. The Prince and Princess then shook hands with me.[39]

In February 1906 they were visited by their old friend Douglas Haig, then a Major General and Inspector of Indian Cavalry. They had great discussions about cavalry training and Bertram helped to write Haig's new training manual.[40] At the start of the hot season in April 1906, Mittie went home to see the children and returned in October along with Mittie's sister Mary who stayed for several months. Bertram was able to get home leave for a short stay in May.[41]

In January 1907, the regiment was inspected at Agra by the Viceroy of India, Lord Minto, who was entertaining the Emir of Afghanistan.[42] The purpose was to maintain friendly relations with the Emir and to deter Russian influence in his country. This was the most important event of Bertram's time at Meerut.

In 1906, Bertram had been thinking about retiring from the army but Douglas Haig persuaded him to stay another year.[43] However, he was on a four-year contract which was coming to an end in 1907 and he decided to go.[44] There were to be cuts in army expenditure and

Fig. 20. Inspection of the 17th Lancers by the Viceroy of India at Agra, January 1907.

manpower.[45] As he had been appointed to the rank of colonel at a relatively young age there were more senior colonels ahead of him in the queue and his prospects of advancement were poor.[46] He therefore took seven months leave to England to avoid the hot season in India before resigning his commission.[47]

When they left, all the officers escorted them to the station, some of them riding the six horses drawing their carriage. There was a great crowd at the station. Nearly all the regiment was there and the band was playing. They took with them three parrots for the children and the head of a crocodile Bertram had shot in a hunting expedition.[48]

They arrived home at the end of May.[49] Bertram was then 41 with three children under the age of seven which was not compatible with foreign postings. He had put his family first.

CHAPTER 6

A COUNTRY GENTLEMAN, 1907-1914

When Bertram and Mittie returned from India the family took up residence at Southington House, just to the west of Overton village, which had been vacated by his elder brother William Wyndham Portal.[1] It was to be their family home for the next forty years. It was modest in comparison to Malshanger or Laverstoke House, being a

Fig. 21. Southington House from the east in 2021.

Georgian house with later additions set in a large garden extending north to the River Test with fishing rights.[2] It accommodated the family, a governess and seven living-in domestic servants.[3]

Margaret (Moggy) was born in 1908 to be followed by Sophie in 1910 and Cecilia in 1911. There were then six children. The eldest and only boy, Melville, was at Wellington House, a boarding prep school at Westgate on Sea in Kent.[4] The older girls were educated at home by a governess.[5] The children's nurse, Nan Jagg, had been with the family since they were in Ireland in 1901.[6]

By August 1907 Bertram was employed at Laverstoke Mill.[7] His two elder brothers, William and Spencer, were the partners in what was then a private family business. William was the senior partner but he had many other interests and the direction of the mill was in Spencer's hands.[8] Bertram's army career gave him no experience of manufacturing or commerce so they drew up a contract of employment which made it crystal clear that he was an assistant and not a partner.[9] It did not state his remuneration but his elder brothers came to an agreement with the company lawyer that Bertram would receive a share of the company profits to be decided by the partners.[10] This would have been very unusual for an assistant. It meant, of course, that the partners' share of the profits would be correspondingly reduced. It would appear that Bertram's army pension and other assets were not sufficient for his needs and that his brothers were helping him out. His position in the company remained unchanged until 1914.

It is perhaps unsurprising that, as a former cavalry officer, he would take an interest in hunting and in 1909 he became secretary of the Vine Hunt with their kennels at Quidhampton less than a mile away.[11] There are, however, no reports of him playing polo. For relaxation he took up fishing on his stretch of the River Test, keeping a record of every catch in his fishing book.

He also became involved with the Overton Rifle Club which had been started by his elder brother William.[12] Rifle clubs were being established all over the country, the intention being that if there were to be a war, army recruits would already know how to shoot.[13] He

Fig. 22. Bertram (left) and Lord Hatherton (right) with fishing gear and Mittie with the children, Southington House, c1908.

joined the Hampshire Territorial Army Association and by 1910 had become chairman of the Western Division, working hard to boost recruitment.[14]

He also immersed himself in local affairs. One of the first things he did was to take charge of the Overton Working Men's Club, started by his uncle Robert 36 years before. It had been closed for repairs and at the re-opening he assured the members he would do everything possible to promote its welfare.[15]

He also became a Justice of the Peace, sitting every month from April 1909.[16] The following year Col. Portal was elected chairman of Overton Parish Council which was much concerned with a proposal for a fire engine, the parish pumps and the state of the roads.[17]

The garden at Southington House was in regular use for fetes which raised money for causes that Bertram and Mittie supported, including the National School, the Overton Conservative Association and the church tower fund.[18] The Overton cricket team played there and he became their president in 1910.[19] Bertram was living the life of a country

GARDEN FÊTE

TO BE HELD

In the Grounds of SOUTHINGTON,

On THURSDAY, AUGUST 12th, 1909,

2.30 to 9.30,

In aid of Overton Church Tower Fund.

⟶ PROGRAMME. ⟵

2.30. **BAND AND ROUNDABOUTS.**

3.0. **MAYPOLE DANCE & FOLK SONGS** (In Garden).

3.45. **¼-MILE FLAT RACE. Inter-Village Competition.**

1st Prize value £2 ; given by Sir William Portal, Bart.
2nd and 3rd Prizes given by Colonel B. Portal.
Entries to be sent to G. L. Bush, Esq., Overton.

4.15. **BICYCLE GYMKHANA. Entrance Fee, 2d.**

(Prizes given by C. Holding, Esq.)

Fig. 23. Programme for a fete, 1909.

gentleman, maintaining his army connections but actively involved with every village activity, just as his father had done.

Bertram also supported the Boy Scouts. He employed William Fairchild, his former 'personal servant' from the army, as his coachman.[20] Fairchild fell in love with the laundry maid at Southington House and, when they married, Bertram provided them with a house. Fairchild was very interested in young people and proposed a Boy Scout troop in the village. It was needed because the parish council was receiving complaints about the nuisance caused by boys playing football and throwing stones in the streets after dark.[21] Col. Portal knew Robert Baden Powell from his time in Edinburgh and he supported this venture. Baden Powell had set up the first experimental scout camp on Brownsea Island in Poole Harbour in August 1907 and his 'Scouting for Boys' was published in 1908.

In 1909, William Fairchild organised a scout camp at Atherfield Chine, a place on the coast four miles east of St Catherine's Point on the Isle of Wight.

The party, numbering 20, were conveyed to Micheldever Station in a motor and traps. The boys have worked exceedingly hard all the summer in a large garden which they hired to raise the necessary funds but, owing to the bad season, the venture has not been very successful, and had not kind friends come to the rescue, the camp would have had to be postponed.[22]

The boys marched eight miles from Newport railway station and were then shown how to pitch their tents. During the week they saw St Catherine's lighthouse, a rocket life-saving apparatus and the Atherfield Lifeboat and they went to sea in a mackerel boat, all the party rowing and fishing together. There was a cricket match against local boys and they swam every day. They returned tanned and brown 'so that their mothers hardly recognised them'.[23]

The following year Robert Baden Powell reviewed the Scout troops in the Basingstoke district. Mr Fairchild was there with 18 Overton Scouts. Bertram also attended as Commissioner for the Kingsclere Division.[24]

Fig. 24. Overton Scouts at Atherfield Chine, 1909.

In 1911, the Scouts raised money to build a Scout hut at Southington House. Mittie helped by organising a concert and coached Charlotte, Hytie and Melville to sing three songs in the programme. It was noted that 'the efforts of Col. Portal, Mr Fairchild and Dr Holding in training the boys have been so far successful'.[25] Bertram was clearly a 'hands-on' supporter.

And so life continued, pleasantly enough, until March 1914 when Bertram received a letter from the War Office,

> Sir, I am commanded by the Army Council to inform you that you have been selected for duty, on general mobilisation, as a Remount Officer (Foreign Commission). You are hereby required, should a general mobilization be ordered, to report yourself immediately and in writing to the Director of Remounts, War Office, when the necessary instructions will be issued to you. This communication must be regarded as *strictly secret* under the Official Secrets Act 1911.[26]

As a reserve officer Bertram was liable for call-up in the event of war. In peacetime, the army bought enough horses for its immediate needs but in war, when horses as well as men would be killed, it required tens of thousands of 'remounts'. It was sensible for the army to employ him to buy horses on its behalf as he was a retired cavalry officer, a polo expert and a huntsman. It also avoided having to divert serving officers from the front line. The Official Secrets Act was rushed through Parliament in 1911 in response to the perceived military threat from Germany and concerns about espionage.

War was declared on 4th August 1914. Anticipating that there would be hardship for families when men were called up, Bertram immediately called a public meeting to consider forming a relief committee but before the meeting happened he had already gone.[27]

CHAPTER 7

IRELAND AND THE EASTER RISING IN DUBLIN, 1914-1916

B ertram must have reported in immediately when war was declared on 4th August. Two days later he received a letter from the War Office to say that he would probably be going to Canada. This was confirmed on 8th August.

> Sir, I am directed to inform you that you have been selected for duty with the remount purchasing division in Canada under Major General F. W. Benson. I am requested to inform you that you are to hold yourself in readiness to sail on or about the 19th. Your pay will be at the rate of 24s. 6d. per day.[1]

The Remount Service requisitioned 140,000 horses in Britain within 12 days of the outbreak of war but needed more.[2]

On 10th August he learned that he would sail from Liverpool on the 16th bound for Quebec aboard the *Grampian* but on the 12th he received a telegram cancelling his deployment. On the 20th he received another telegram, 'Proceed at once to Curragh on appointment to 8th Reserve Cavalry'.[3]

THE CURRAGH

The Curragh Camp was a British military base about 30 miles south west of Dublin. Someone at the War Office had realized that he was capable of more than buying horses and had lived in Ireland. Seventeen Reserve Cavalry Regiments were formed by the British Army on the outbreak of war. They were training and not combat formations, their purpose being to train replacements for the active regiments on the Western Front. The 8th Reserve Cavalry Brigade trained men for the 16th and 17th Lancers, as well as the Dorsetshire and Oxfordshire Yeomanry.[4]

At first Bertram lived at Ponsonby Barracks at the Curragh Camp but then managed to rent a house. When Mittie saw it she realised it was not big enough for the whole family so 'the nursery party would have to stay at Teddesley Hall'.[5] The nursery party consisted of Moggy, Sophie, Cecilia and Nan Jagg. Mittie often travelled to Shropshire to see them. Mr Fairchild was brought from Southington and he was instructed to bring the car, the children's pony and the dog over to Ireland. Southington House was shut up and Belgian refugees were put into Fairchild's house.[6]

Fig. 25. Bertram with Melville, Charlotte and Hyacinthe at the Curragh Camp.

By December 1915, Bertram had found another house large enough for the whole family. However, there are indications that Bertram was in financial difficulties at this time. Bertram wrote in a letter to Melville at Eton College that 'we all have to be very careful with money now'.[7] This was probably because he was no longer receiving anything from the family paper business since he was not living near the mill or doing any work for the partners. His army pay would not have covered the expense of maintaining the family in Ireland.

Nevertheless, he was quite clear about where his duty lay. When a young family friend was killed in the trenches in November 1914, he wrote, 'I feel sure that these dreadful things are happening to teach us all a lesson and remember that you must do your duty in that state to which it has pleased God to call you'.[8]

As a result of Lord Kitchener's appeal for volunteers, there was a flood of new recruits to be trained which kept Bertram very busy. The 17th Lancers were receiving recruits at the rate of 200 a day until the regiment numbered over 2,000. No adequate provision had been made for accommodation, food or clothing but in a fortnight these problems had been solved and horses had been procured by the end of August.[9] Training lasted eight months and was a mix of drilling, marching, musketry and divisional maneouvres.[10]

In October 1914, Bertram was instructed to receive 150 more recruits but there was nowhere left at the Curragh Camp to accommodate them. When men were trained they were sent to France but Bertram commented, 'I don't expect they need so many cavalry now as they have not been doing much lately. Most of the men I have sent are still at the base in France'.[11] By that time the war had become static and cavalry regiments had no role in trench warfare. In December, Bertram wrote to a colleague on the Western Front to say he thought it was unnecessary to train cavalry recruits to use a sword. The reply indicated that no-one would care if they could or not.[12]

Many of the recruits were Irish. A bill for Irish Home Rule finally passed into law in March 1914 but there was widespread support in Ireland for the British war aims and Home Rule was deferred until the end of the war.[13] Over the course of the war more than 130,000 Irishmen volunteered to serve in the British army. They were not only from Ulster but also from Connaught, Munster, Leinster and Dublin. By the end of 1915, nearly 17,000 Dubliners were serving.[14] For some, however, Home Rule was not enough. They wanted to sever all links with Britain and establish a republic by armed rebellion if necessary. British Intelligence estimated that in early 1916 there were at least 4,500 men trained and armed to fight for this cause.[15] Of these, 2,665 were in Dublin.[16]

By August 1915, Bertram was second in command of all the troops at the Curragh under Brigadier General W.H.M. Lowe, including the 3rd Reserve Cavalry Brigade.[17] In September they were inspected by General Friend, Commander in Chief of the British Forces in Ireland. Bertram wrote,

> I had the whole lot on parade except the gunners, 2,574 was the total. It was a lovely day and we had massed bands, a march past and a short field day afterwards. Gen. Friend was delighted and wants me to take a tour round Ireland to help recruiting and to impress the pro-Germans. I should like to do it but I fear it will be too late in the year.[18]

At about this time the British Admiralty was receiving intelligence of an intended shipment of arms from Germany to Irish republicans to coincide with an uprising. General Friend organized 'a small mobile force which would be available at a moment's notice, to repel a landing … or to assist the Civil Power in the major cities'.[19] The 'mobile force' was part of Bertram's 3rd Cavalry Brigade.[20] It was an idea based on the mobile columns of the Boer War using the rail network. In order to move quickly their horses would be left at the Curragh.

Like Bertram, Generals Friend and Lowe were veterans of the Boer War which had some similarities to the threat they faced in Ireland. With modern weapons supplied by Germany, the small land-locked Boer Republics had taken on the might of the British Empire and in the first year, with an irregular and mainly un-uniformed army of farmers, they had succeeded in causing severe embarrassment to the

British. There had even been an Irish brigade fighting on the side of the Boers. Their experienced veterans were amongst those planning a rebellion.[21]

General Friend had evidently judged that Bertram's troops were the most effective force available to him in Ireland. Conscription was introduced in January 1916. Because of the sensitivity about Irish Home Rule it did not apply to Ireland, but it would have resulted in another flood of men from the rest of Britain to be trained at the Curragh.

THE EASTER RISING IN DUBLIN, APRIL 1916

On 15th April, General Friend received Admiralty intelligence that German ships carrying arms and ammunition had already left for Ireland and that an uprising was planned 'no later than Easter Saturday, 22nd April'.[22] He passed the information to the authorities at Dublin Castle and to the Curragh Camp where all leave for officers was cancelled.[23] The German ships were intercepted and when Easter Saturday and Sunday passed without incident it seemed that the plans for a rising had been abandoned.

At 12 noon on Easter Monday, 24th April, armed rebels of the Irish Volunteers, the Irish Citizen Army and the Republican Brotherhood occupied the General Post Office in Dublin and buildings at many locations north and south of the River Liffey. The rebels outnumbered the British troops available in the city and the civil and military authorities in Dublin were caught out. They knew an uprising was planned but there was disagreement about what action to take. They were so focussed on recruitment for the British army and the issue of Home Rule that they were reluctant to antagonise republican sympathisers by arresting their leaders. Firm information that a rising would happen in Dublin at the Easter week-end was discounted and their intention was to arrest the rebel leaders after the holiday. They were still seeking approval from London when they found themselves trapped in the Castle by rebel gunmen.[24]

When the alarm was raised at the Curragh the 3rd Cavalry Brigade were finishing the preparations for their regimental sports in the afternoon and Bertram had gone home to receive guests for lunch.[25] The first indication of trouble was a telephone message from military headquarters in Dublin received by the duty staff officer, Major Salt, that 'the mobile column might be needed in a day or two'. It was followed by the news that the Sinn Féiners had occupied the General Post Office and buildings around Dublin Castle. (The British always called the rebels 'Sinn Féiners'. This was inaccurate as Sinn Féin was then a small republican political party opposed to the rebellion.) At 12.35pm the order came through by telephone, 'Mobile Column to proceed at once to Dublin by train'. Salt ordered the gun at the Curragh to be fired twice which was the signal for the Mobile Column to 'stand to'.[26] The arrangements for transporting 1,500 troops with their weapons, ammunition, food and everything they needed were 'according to a pre-arranged plan'.[27] Bertram was on the first train to leave the Curragh siding at 3.30pm. He had bought sandwiches from the station buffet because he had received a message that the headquarters staff in Dublin had no food.

He had with him an Army Correspondence Book 152, Field Service, and used it to write a daily diary.[28] He knew that when it was all over he would be required to write reports and his diary contains all the information he would need. His entries are short and factual with all the signs of being written in a great hurry. Bertram started writing on the train. 'No idea whether we shall have a clear run to Dublin or not'. He also wrote, 'Salt took Ponsonby's place at the station – a very fortunate exchange'. Salt was 'eager for promotion' whereas Ponsonby was more concerned to preserve his position as Master of Hounds of the Curragh.[29] Major Sir Thomas Salt, Bt became Bertram's staff officer for the best part of the action that followed. He also wrote a diary and it is clear that they became good friends.[30] He was 2nd Baronet Salt, of Standon, Staffordshire not far from Teddesley Hall.

Bertram must have been acutely aware that a train packed with soldiers would be an admirable target for an ambush and he did not know whether the rebels held the Kingsbridge station terminus or not. However, when the train arrived at 4.30pm they were unopposed although much firing could be heard nearby. It was just under four hours since the alarm had been raised. Bertram was met by a staff officer with orders to send 800 men to the Castle, including a machine gun section. City Hall, just to the north of the Castle, was eventually taken from the rebels long after dark.[31] Detachments we also sent to the Viceregal Lodge and other locations. An officer in plain clothes was sent into the city to see what he could find out about rebel positions.[32]

Bertram then reported to the British Military Headquarters at the Royal Hospital nearby. The first thing he learned was that General Friend had gone on leave a few days before. Friend had told his staff officers in Dublin that he was going but they had not told anyone else. By this time the rebels at the G.P.O. had cut the telephone lines to the provinces. Lowe had sent a dispatch rider by motor cycle seeking information so Bertram sent him straight back to the Curragh to tell General Lowe that he was the most senior officer in Ireland. Lowe then decided he must come to Dublin himself.[33]

The only information available was that the rebels held the G.P.O. and a portion of Dublin Castle but their numbers were unknown. Bertram wrote, 'The troops in Dublin seem to be scattered about without any definite plan and no communication between them except by telephone'. It was suspected that the local Dublin telephone exchange was being tapped by the rebels.[34] Bertram wrote that 'a plan for occupying the streets was carefully discussed but no-one at H.Q. had much experience of street-fighting. The main principle seems to be to occupy corner houses with a commanding view'. Though Bertram's mobile column had been formed in case of insurrection 'in the major cities', it is clear that neither he nor anyone else had given any thought about *how* they would have to fight. The plan for getting troops to Dublin seems to have been excellent but the cavalry brigade was trained to fight on horseback against an organised army in open country. Few of the men had ever been in action before and they had no training in street-fighting. In contrast, James Conolly, the commander of the rebel forces in Dublin and a Boer war veteran, had published a series of eight detailed articles on the subject in the *Workers' Republic* in 1915 and had trained the Citizen Army in the tactics of urban warfare. The civil authorities at Dublin Castle certainly knew about the *Workers' Republic* but had not suppressed it.[35] Had Conolly's articles been seen by the military intelligence officers in Dublin they would have learned that in street-fighting the defenders are always at an advantage because the attackers are more exposed. They would have learned much about concealment, holding fire until the enemy is at close range, the intelligent use of barricades and tunnelling through the internal walls of terraced houses. Connolly provided historical examples of small numbers of 'citizen soldiers' in well prepared positions holding off or even defeating greatly superior regular forces, inflicting heavy casualties.[36] There had been a serious failure of intelligence, planning and training on the British side and it would cost them dearly.

Bertram returned to Kingsbridge station and managed some sleep until General Lowe arrived at 4.30am bringing 856 infantry, three machine guns and 665 bombs from the Curragh.[37] By 7am he

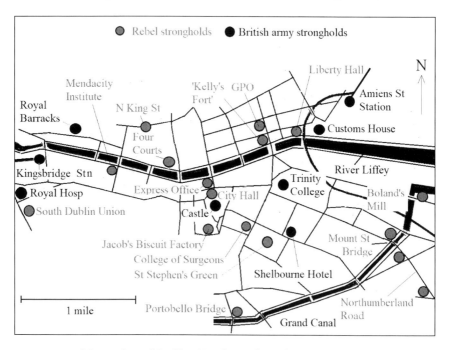

Map 7. Central Dublin, Tuesday 25th April 1916. There were more rebel strongpoints south of the river than are shown here.

had gathered enough information about where the rebel and British strongholds were to formulate a plan. There were isolated bodies of British troops at Kingsbridge Station, the Castle and the Customs House. Trinity College had also been held. The first thing to do was to join them up and Bertram was given the task of creating a safe passage from Kingsbridge Station to the Castle.[38]

Bertram moved through back streets with an advance guard of 14 men who occupied cross-roads and corner houses. Then another party advanced beyond them until they were used up and the same process was repeated until whole streets were occupied. The men went in single file close to the walls on both sides. They arrived at the Castle without any casualties having advanced about one and a half miles in two hours leaving the whole route occupied behind them. Bertram was taking the greatest care to minimise the risk to his men from snipers and he led from the front. It was very fortunate that there were no rebel strongholds along their route.

The Castle and City Hall had already been cleared of rebels but dangerous fire was coming from a red house at the south east corner of Parliament Street, across the road from City Hall. The Daily Express building on the south west corner was incorrectly believed to be unoccupied and Bertram decided to take it with a detachment of 20 men of the Royal Dublin Fusiliers. They were covered by fire from the front of City Hall and bombs thrown from the roof. Unfortunately, 'the door of the Daily Express building was much tougher than it looked and took about half a minute to break. During that time seven men who were forcing the door were 'stretched out on the pavement'.[39] Bertram had learned that it was extremely dangerous for a crowd of men to be in the open even for a short time. Once the door was forced, three more waves of attackers were sent in. A firefight ensued within the building which eventually fell to the British.[40]

Though the fight for the Express Office was continuing, Bertram took the initiative to push on to Trinity College. It had always been a loyal Unionist institution and was a better choice as a base for operations than Dublin Castle. It was enclosed by very substantial walls and from the upper storeys there was a direct view up Sackville Street (now

O'Connell Street) towards the G.P.O. while Liberty Hall, the Citizen Army headquarters, was only a quarter of a mile away across the river.[41]

When firing was heard at Trinity College from across the river at noon on Monday, the gates were closed and the headquarters building of the Officer Training Corps was sandbagged. They had about 300 rifles with ammunition and prepared to defend the College from the rebels. By nightfall about 40 officer cadets had reported in for duty. The next morning there was heavy sniper fire from rebels to the west and north of the college and on the railway viaduct, some from only 30 yards away. The officer cadets returned fire with such effect that the rebels believed it was more strongly defended than it actually was and they did not attempt to storm the grounds.[42]

Elsie Mahaffy, the Provost's daughter, saw it all from their house in the grounds. She wrote in her account,

> After lunch I climbed to the highest-up room in the Provost's House, the only one we have looking into College Green and facing the Bank of Ireland. This great thoroughfare was utterly deserted except for the occasional ambulance waggon darting across it. On the roof of Trinity College, sheltered by its stone parapet, about 50 Trinity College men fired occasionally up Dame St and were at once answered by rebel snipers on the roofs of the street. In fact they seemed to be on every roof in the town. How I longed for the arrival of soldiers …
>
> About 4 o'clock, to my intense relief, I heard at last the regular march of soldiers. Looking down, I saw below in the street a multitude of khaki-clad men coming into College. So I flew down to hear some news.
>
> In the Library with my father I found Col. Portal, Capt. Longroft and one or two more soldiers who had arrived into Trinity College to use it as a base for operations in our division of Dublin. To take the G.P.O. and capture the rebel leaders there and to blow up Liberty Hall were the objects placed before Col. Portal. He appeared to me, as well as being an elegant English gentleman, to be remarkably able. He had never been to Dublin before and was entirely ignorant even of the street names.
>
> His first enquiries were for a map of Dublin and a high view from

which he could prospect his field of action and he asked my father's advice as to where he ought to place the '18-pounder' to blow down Liberty Hall. A good map of the streets showed him all he wanted to learn and, having laid plans for the big guns next morning, he got his men billeted in College and returned to tea and later on to dine with us.[43]

On Tuesday evening Bertram knew that he would be assigned an area which included the rebel headquarters at the G.P.O. and Liberty Hall. Reinforcements from England and Belfast began to arrive during the night.[44]

On Wednesday Bertram's task was to destroy Liberty Hall, the headquarters of the Irish Citizen Army. It was thought to be strongly held and to contain large stores of ammunition and supplies. Many soldiers' lives could be saved by destroying the building with artillery shells.

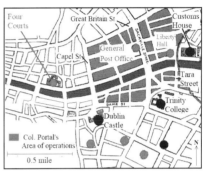

Map 8. Col. Portal's assigned area is shown in grey.

Elsie Mahaffy heard the noise of heavy guns being brought into Trinity College very early on Wednesday morning with many men driving the mules. 'The pounding down of Liberty Hall lasted over half an hour and the foundations of the Provost's house trembled'.[45] Meanwhile Bertram's troops were advancing along Tara Street which enabled him to place a field gun at its northern end, directly opposite Liberty Hall.

> A gun boat in the river was to co-operate. Everything worked splendidly and Liberty Hall was practically blown to pieces but the place was empty. They must have known of our arrangements. There was continuous firing from a house at south west corner of Sackville St which is Kelly's shop. We got a gun onto it from inside Trinity College walls and blew the shop to pieces. Communication is now established with the Customs House and therefore between Customs House and Kingsbridge Station.[46]

There is a detail of this operation not mentioned in Bertram's diary. When a field gun is fired there is a tremendous recoil. The trail of the gun carriage has a spade-shaped projection which is sunk into the ground to prevent the carriage from hurtling backwards when the gun is fired. This cannot be done in a city street. The audacious solution was to send a party of officer cadets from Trinity College in workmen's clothes in advance of the action to lift some of the cobbles with crowbars at the north end of the street. They were in full view of Liberty Hall but it was thought they were dealing with a gas leak.[47]

That evening Bertram was summoned to H.Q. at 9.30pm and a staff car was sent to collect him. On the journey he had a narrow escape. British soldiers guarding the route failed to recognise the car in the dark and opened fire. The driver stopped the car and yelled 'Friend!' and about a dozen nervous young soldiers allowed them to proceed.[48]

At the conference Bertram found General Friend, General Lowe, their headquarters staff and his own commanding officers. The reason it was held so late in the evening was probably because of other events during the day. Troops arriving from Belfast and Templemore had completed a ring round the city centre north of the River Liffey. The southern ring was not yet complete because two battalions of the Sherwood Foresters, who had just arrived from England, were held up by heavy fire in Northumberland Avenue near Mount Street Bridge (see Map 7). They were ordered to make frontal attacks over open ground against rebel positions which were to be taken 'at all costs'.[49] By nightfall the Foresters had prevailed but to clear just one street, 30 British soldiers had been killed and 130 wounded. There were not many more than 20 rebel defenders altogether.[50] With a better understanding of street fighting such heavy casualties could have been avoided.

The plan for further operations was 'General Lowe's entirely'.[51] General Friend had returned to Dublin the previous day and was nominally in command but Lord Kitchener, Secretary of State for War, had already appointed General Maxwell to replace him because of his absence when the rebellion started.[52] Friend allowed Lowe to continue what he had started pending the arrival of his successor. The main attack would not be delivered until the troops from England could reinforce the troops at Trinity College and the Castle'.[53] Then Bertram's troops were to surround the area around Sackville Street and the G.P.O. so that the rebels could not escape.

The attack on the rebel H.Q. was likely to be the toughest fight of all. Bertram would command detachments of the 5th Leinsters and the 3rd Royal Irish Regiment from the Curragh, plus the 2/6 Battalion of the Sherwood Foresters from England and an Ulster Composite Battalion when they were ready for action.[54] They were all infantry regiments. It was a measure of General Lowe's confidence in him as a reserve cavalry officer from a training brigade that he was to command infantry. Bertram did not know them or their officers and had no way of assessing their capabilities before leading them in action.

Bertram was assigned 'two improvised armoured motors consisting of large circular boilers mounted on top of Guinness' lorries'.[55] He did not write in his diary that this was his own idea.[56] It probably came to him when he reflected on seven of his men being 'laid out on the pavement' on Tuesday afternoon. Here was a way of protecting the lives of his men from snipers and making progress against the rebels but to be any use it would have to be done in great haste.

On the morning of Wednesday 26th April the Board of Directors at the Guinness brewery near Kingsbridge Station received a message to say that a Major Deasy had been in touch by telephone with a request to convert the Guinness flat-bed lorries they had already lent to the British army into armoured vehicles. Permission was granted by A. E. Guinness the same day.[57] Major Henry Deasy was Bertram's quartermaster who could not have taken this step on his own initiative.[58]

The next question was where to source armour plate for the conversion. Bertram knew all about the armoured trains used by the British in the Boer War.[59] Henry Deasy, who was born in Dublin and founded a car manufacturing company in 1906, would have known to go to the Inchicore railway workshops about two miles from Kingsbridge Station where locomotives were assembled.[60] What could they provide that would be very quick to assemble?

Fig 26. Armoured lorry showing the smoke box door.

The work was carried out there using locomotive smoke-boxes (not boilers) bolted together. The one at the back had a ready-made door. It is not clear who designed them though it was very probably only a rough sketch.[61]

It is clear that nobody waited for permission from Guinness. At midday Major Salt took delivery of the prototype vehicle and drove it to Kingsbridge Station to be inspected. Some minor modifications were proposed and Salt returned to Inchicore for the work to be done. By evening a second vehicle had been finished.[62]

Five of these armoured lorries were built.[63] They could carry up to 20 men and we would call them the world's first armoured personnel carriers.[64] Their first use in combat was on Thursday morning.[65] It is quite remarkable that from first concept to design, assembly and deployment in battle took only 24 hours.

The attack began early on Thursday morning and Bertram left Trinity College to establish his headquarters at the portico of City Hall which was well protected from snipers and afforded a clear view down Parliament Street to Grattan Bridge and Capel Street over the river.[66]

The bridge was under fire from buildings across the river with no cover of any kind. The armoured lorries went backwards and forwards over the bridge ferrying groups of about 20 men from the Castle with tools to break down the doors of the occupied houses. The use of the armoured lorries in the taking of Capel Street was recorded by one of the Sherwood Foresters.

An armoured lorry took one officer and 18 other ranks and rushed them to a corner house. Here half the party was dropped and they quickly opened fire from the top windows. The other half of the party was dropped at the corner opposite and the men rushed in and occupied the top rooms. A good field of fire was thus obtained in either direction and the task of picking off snipers was carried out with gusto. When all these corner posts had been occupied the companies marched out into the street and were given instructions to barricade all side streets on either side of Capel Street.[67]

Major Salt recorded that

Hardly any bullets hit the armoured car and those that did made no impression on it whatever. The 5th Leinster Regiment worked in this way for 1200 yards up Capel Street and then our cordon line swung to the right along Gt Britain Street and other regiments took over the work. It was carried on the same way with the armoured lorry. Meanwhile, another cordon line was being thrown out on the other side of our square area and this eventually met our line at the top of Sackville Street. Then the cordon was complete.[68]

Bertram had learned about the use of barricades from the rebels. He commented that the armoured lorries 'were of the greatest assistance, not only in saving life but also in enabling the streets to be occupied very quickly'.[69] The cordon around the Sackville Street area had been completed 'with small loss'.[70] By nightfall the rebels at the Four Courts were separated from those at the G.P.O. It was a brilliantly successful operation. In a few hours the principal British strategic objective had been achieved and the eventual defeat of the rebels was now certain. Judging by what had happened at Mount Street Bridge we can conclude that without the armoured lorries it could have taken several days with immense loss of life.

Another operation was mounted the same evening. Bertram had received word that on Monday, before the rebellion started, the 6th Reserve Cavalry Regiment had sent an escort of two officers and about 50 men to fetch some bombs and cases containing several hundred rifles from the North Wall docks. On the way back they had to pass the Four Courts which by then had been occupied by the rebels. The wagons had to be left in the open in Charles Street and some of the men got into cover in the neighbouring buildings only a few yards from the Four Courts where they stayed with hardly any food (see Map 7). They urgently needed to be rescued and Bertram sent the armoured lorry to get the men out. They also brought back the bombs, but the wagons containing the heavy cases of rifles had to be left. The officer in charge of the convoy had shot himself and his body had to be left too.

The next morning Bertram put Major Salt in command of an audacious operation to bring back the rifles lest they should be taken by the rebels. Major Salt wrote,

> The armoured lorry went down three times to Charles Street. The first time it dragged back one of the wagons with the cases of rifles. Only one man was wounded by a bullet that came into the armoured car through a loophole. The second and third times I went in command of the lorry. We went forward down Parliament Street and over the bridge. Then we backed slowly along the quay to Charles Street holding a big iron plate over the big machine gun loophole through which the man had been wounded the time before… The driver could not see where he was going when he started backing the lorry, so I kept glued to a loophole watching the edge of the pavement to direct him… We were exposed to fire along the quay, along which we had to back very slowly. Once in Charles Street cover was obtained and we were not fired at there. We backed the lorry into it and got into safer

ground... The first time I went out we only took men to occupy the houses on each side of Charles Street near the wagons so as to prevent the rebels from getting at them... The last time we went out we took a party to turn round the wagon which was facing the wrong way and to rope it on to the back of the armoured lorry and a couple of men with a stretcher to fetch the body of the dead officer...

Just before we turned into Charles Street, a bullet came right through the side, rather below a loophole. It was the only one that had pierced the metal and it luckily did very little harm. Of course, crowded as we were inside, a bullet coming in could hardly fail to hit somebody, but this one grazed the face of one man and hit another in the hand. As soon as we were far enough down Charles Street, we threw open the door again... The ones for the wagon swung it round and tied it with ropes to the back of the armoured lorry and the two with the stretcher brought out the body of the dead officer. I never saw men work faster... We returned to the Castle at a good pace, dragging the loaded wagon behind us.[71]

The principal task on Friday 28th was to close the two lines of the cordon inwards till they reached Marlborough Street and Denmark Street where they stopped to avoid the possibility of the attackers firing at each other.

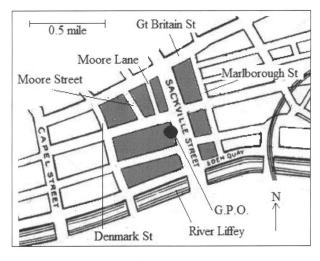

Map 9. Central Dublin, 5pm on Friday 28th April.

Bertram was then given the 2/5 and 2/6 battalions of the South Staffordshire Regiment to begin a second movement to invest the Four Courts. At this point he moved his headquarters back to the Castle. Because of the success with the armoured lorries the previous day it may have been thought that this would be easy. North King Street was chosen as the northern boundary as it was incorrectly believed to be beyond the area occupied by the rebels. The armoured lorries were used again but the rebels had erected barricades across the streets and the encircling movement was not fully completed by dark. The lorries could not be used at night as they had no lights.[72] The maze of narrow streets provided ideal cover for the rebels. General Maxwell wrote later that, apart from the action at Mount Street Bridge, 'this was by far the worst fighting that occurred in the whole of Dublin. At first, the troops, coming from one end of the street, were repulsed, and it was only when we made an attack from both ends that we succeeded after twenty-four hours' fighting in capturing the street'.[73] The Staffordshires had to resort to the rebel tactic of breaking through the walls of adjacent houses. British casualties were heavy. Twelve were killed and 28 wounded in this action. The armoured lorries had their limitations.[74]

At 7am on Saturday Bertram visited all his commanding officers and the encirclement of the Four Courts was completed two hours later. Huge fires were raging in Sackville Street resulting from an artillery bombardment from Trinity College, which restricted the area occupied by the rebels. At noon Bertram was in the thick of the fighting at a British barricade at the top of Moore Street, just to the west of Sackville Street, where he sent this message to General Lowe.

We have been engaged with the Sinn Féiners in Moore Street and from reliable information received … about 100 Sinn Féiners are located in a white house at the southern end of Moor Lane. I ordered the gunner officer to put five shells into the house and as a result a Red Cross nurse of the enemy has come in with a verbal message from the self-called Commandant Pearse, Republican Forces, to the effect that he wishes to treat with the commandant of forces. We have detained the nurse here and are proceeding with the operations of searching and closing in.[75]

General Lowe came down and together they wrote a letter to P. H. Pearse and sent the nurse back with it, saying that the surrender must be absolutely unconditional. Presently she brought back a letter from Pearse who wished for better terms. They wrote another letter repeating that the surrender must be unconditional. Soon afterwards Pearse and the nurse returned, Pearse surrendered himself and he was driven away. Firing had already ceased and a general cease-fire followed.[76] The nurse was Elizabeth O'Farrell.[77]

Bertram and his troops spent the rest of the day rounding up 448 prisoners and collecting their weapons. That night he returned to the Castle where there was nothing to eat except army rations of bully beef and biscuits but he managed a full night's sleep for the first time since the rebellion had started.

On Sunday he and General Lowe negotiated the surrender of the rebels elsewhere in the city through some Franciscan Friars who acted as intermediaries. By the end of the day about 1,300 rebels had been detained.

Fig. 27. Burning ruins in Upper Sackville Street.

Fig 28. The provost of Trinity College observing
General Maxwell's inspection at College Green, 1st May.

On Monday 1st May there was a parade at Trinity College of the Officer Cadets and the six regiments under Bertram's command for General Maxwell's inspection and commendation.

After lunch with the Provost of Trinity College, Bertram spent the afternoon writing his report.[78] On the same day, Generals Maxwell and Lowe conferred on how to arrest those in the Dublin area who were still holding out and they proposed that Portal should be in command of the area south of the River Liffey.[79] However, they must have changed their minds since he was given a mobile column to search County Mayo. On Tuesday, Bertram and all the troops from the Curragh returned there.[80]

He was given no time to rest. When the fighting was over, General Maxwell reported,

> In other parts of Ireland similar attacks on police posts had been made by armed bands of Sinn Féiners. In order to deal with these, I organised various mobile columns. … Each column was allotted a definite area, which, in close co-operation with the local police, was gone through, and dangerous Sinn Féiners and men who were known to have taken an active part in the rising were arrested.[81]

Fig. 29. Bertram en route to Castlebar with his driver and Fairchild behind him. Bertram had recuited him into the regiment.

Martial law had been declared and Maxwell had the power to instruct the police. His intention as the fighting ended was to arrest 'all known or suspected Sinn Féiners'.[82] However, his orders to the column commanders on May 5th were that 'only the dangerous ones' were to be arrested.[83] Colonel Portal was to command Mobile Column No 4 which left the Curragh on Thursday 4th May. By that afternoon he was in Castlebar, County Mayo in the west of Ireland.

His 'flying column' consisted of 165 cavalrymen, 449 infantry, 30 artillerymen and a field gun along with 716 horses. Having interviewed the Inspector of Police and the Chief Constable, Bertram sent a message to Dublin to say that it would make sense for him to search County Sligo as well as County Mayo. This was agreed and Bertram made arrangements with the local police to send detachments of his cavalry with police to arrest prominent Sinn Féiners in Castlebar, Westport, Ballina and Sligo.[84]

The intended role of the military was to assist the police in making arrests, 'being nearby in case of a hostile demonstration by the inhabitants', and to transport those who were charged to Dublin. The police would decide who to arrest from their local knowledge.

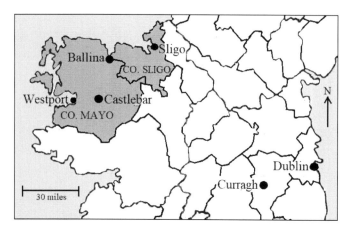

Map 10. County Mayo and County Sligo.

However, there followed several days of confusion about which men should be detained. The next instruction from General Maxwell's staff officers in Dublin was that it was only those who had 'borne arms in the insurrection' which did not apply in this area. The local authorities were incensed and telegrams flew back and forth. The next instruction was that 'only those who had illegally borne arms' could be arrested. A further telegram added that the main purpose of the flying columns was 'the moral effect and to search for arms'.

It was clear to Bertram that General Maxwell was trying to minimise the number of arrests whereas the local police were intent on charging those who had supported the republican cause at meetings and parades, whether they themselves had borne arms or not. Bertram thought that searching for guns would be a complete waste of effort and he did not even try.[85] Some weapons and ammunition fell into their hands in the process of making arrests and 20 guns were handed in.[86]

Eventually General Lowe arrived. He agreed with the police and gave permission to charge those who had attended parades in the area. The arrests were finally made on Tuesday 9th May and 18 prisoners were brought in by train from Westport and marched to the jail in Castlebar. Another 16 men were brought in from Sligo. It is clear from the Castlebar prison records that most of those sent to Dublin were 'rank and file'.[87] Maxwell's instructions had been frustrated.

The next day, Bertram instructed the police to arrest Darrell Figgis and P. J. Doris.[88] Figgis had been to Germany in 1914 and had successfully organised a large shipment of arms to Ireland in that year.[89] Doris was charged with 'aiding and abetting preparations for a rebellion'.[90]

On 14th May, Bertram sent a message to Dublin.

> I am sending two more prisoners, Darrell Figgis and P. J. Doris, to Dublin. Both these men are well known and are looked upon as dangerous Sinn Féiners. Doris belongs to Westport and Figgis belongs to Achill. Three of the worst leaders have already been sent to Dublin namely Charles Hughes, Joseph McBride and Joseph Gill. These three, together with Figgis and Doris are the most dangerous Sinn Féiners in Westport district. It is considered most desirable by all those in authority in the district that an example should be made of these men.[91]

Though the decisions had been made by the military, Bertram was careful not to pass judgment on the prisoners himself but to quote the authorities in the area. On the same day he wrote to his son from the Imperial Hotel, Castlebar,

> We are having quite a nice time here. About 50 prisoners have been sent into Dublin for trial and all the people round about here are as quiet as possible. There were two men at the jail here and the Dublin authorities did not think there

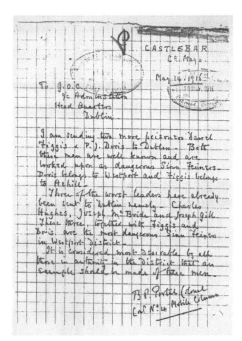

Fig. 30. Message sent from Castlebar.

was enough evidence against them. I was told to release them with a severe caution.

I went to the office in the jail and sat at the table. Major Salt and the County Inspector of Police stood behind me. Then the first man came in – a miserable looking creature – I spoke to him as sternly as I could and told him he had had a very narrow escape and if he ever misbehaved again he would be re-arrested and deported. He promised, by all his Gods, to be good for the future. He looked terrified. I saw the other man in the same way and I don't think either of them will give any further trouble.

I have got a motor and travel all over the country. My column is scattered all over the place. The idea is that the people should see the troops as much as possible. I took the whole column to the town of Westport the other day, about 12 miles away. The people were much impressed and were heard to say, 'They will surely beat the Germans if they have got this number of troops'.[92]

Their work in the area was now done and on 18th May Bertram received orders to move the whole column south to Templemore in County Tipperary. However, there were no arrests to be made there and Bertram had time to enjoy the countryside and go fishing. Eventually it was agreed that his column should be disbanded and they returned to their bases. Bertram arrived home on 22nd May.[93]

Bertram's diary confirms that Maxwell was trying to keep the numbers of arrests down and it was the local police who were keen to detain the rank and file. When the Prime Minister, Herbert Asquith, interviewed prisoners at Richmond Barracks he was quite clear that many of them should not have been there and it was the local police who had been 'over-zealous'.[94]

Bertram had played a prominent role in supressing the uprising in a few days by adapting very quickly to urban warfare. His armoured lorries did not alter the outcome but they undoubtedly shortened the conflict and thereby saved many lives on both sides. Bertram never commented on the rebels in his diary. It was simply his account of a job that had to be done.

His exploits in Ireland had not gone unnoticed. On the day after the surrender General Maxwell sent a one-page report to Lord French, Commander in Chief, Home Forces, which concluded, 'When it is over, I will send in full reports but in the meanwhile I would like to state that the greatest credit is due to Major General Friend, Brig. General Lowe and Colonel B. Portal for their excellent dispositions and unflagging energy in dealing with a very difficult situation'.[95]

General Maxwell duly drafted his official dispatch about the rebellion on 23rd May and it was sent to the Prime Minister. In it he wrote, 'On Col. Portal, who led the Dublin Flying Column, lay the difficult task of crushing the rebels in the Sackville Street and Four Courts areas. In dealing with this problem he showed remarkable ability and coolness'.[96]

By the time the dispatch was published in July the draft had been heavily edited by the Cabinet and nearly all commendations of individuals had been removed.[97] By then the Cabinet was well aware that public opinion in Ireland was rapidly turning against them.[98] It was perceived that it would be a political mistake to commend individuals for their achievements during the rebellion.

Nevertheless, Bertram's exploits had been recognised at the highest level. He was honoured by King George V with a C.B. (Companion of the Most Honourable Order of the Bath) in January 1917 for his services in Ireland.[99] He wrote that, 'he was pleased about the C.B. but it was far more than he deserved when he saw others who had borne the brunt of the fighting in France'.[100]

During the rising, the people of Dublin appear to have been shocked by and largely opposed to the rebellion. The inhabitants in the area were more intent on looting the shops than helping the rebels.[101] However, while Bertram was at Castlebar, 15 rebels were executed by firing squad after hasty courts-martial that were later recognized to have been conducted illegally. There had also been instances of British soldiers shooting prisoners and the damage to the city caused by incendiary shells had been immense. More than 3,000 people were arrested and 1,600 were interned in English and Welsh gaols, not in Ireland.[102] All of these factors turned Irish public opinion against the British. Those deemed at the time to have been rebels and traitors who had sought help from Germany became patriots, heroes and martyrs.

In the War of Independence that followed in 1919, British forces, especially the notorious 'Black and Tan' auxiliaries, were guilty of a series of disgraceful atrocities in a bitter conflict characterised by murders and reprisals by both sides. The whole period, from 1916 to the creation of the Irish Free State in 1922, came to be regarded on both sides of the Irish Sea as a shameful episode in the history of the British in Ireland.[103] It was a subject best avoided. Bertram's role in suppressing the rebellion in 1916 was entirely honourable but, when his obituary came to be written in 1949, it listed in detail all his military accomplishments except for his role in the Easter Rising for which his C.B. had been awarded.[104] It may have been decided that it would be better not to mention it.

CHAPTER 8

THE WESTERN FRONT, 1916-1918

Bertram was not given long to relax. By the end of May it was confirmed that he would be sent to France. The huge expansion of the British army in 1916 led to a shortage of officers of his rank and those on the Reserve List were used to fill the gaps.

From a purely military standpoint, the Easter Rising had been no more than a small, brief and irritating distraction from the main focus on the Western Front. In 1916 the British held a sector of the front line extending from just north of Ypres to the River Somme, a distance of about 85 miles. Five armies and one and a half million men were under the command of Douglas Haig, by then a Field Marshal. To understand Bertram's story we need to go back to the Boer War, the previous large-scale deployment of the British Army. All the senior commanders in 1914 were veterans of that war and if Bertram had not resigned his commission in 1907 he might have been one of them.

In 1914, many believed that the war would be like the Boer War only bigger. Even before that war had ended, the youthful Winston Churchill foresaw that a future European war 'could only end in the ruin of the vanquished and the exhaustion of the conquerors... a cruel, heart rending struggle, which must demand, perhaps for several years, the whole manhood of the nation and the entire suspension of peaceful industries.'[1] He already understood the concept that we now call 'total war'. By 1914, Lord Kitchener, as Secretary of State for War, knew it too. He was responsible for the massive expansion of the British army and the creation of a munitions industry capable of supporting it. Kitchener had marched from Bloemfontein to Pretoria in 1900 with 43,000 men. In 1914 he persuaded a reluctant Cabinet that Britain needed an army of millions.[2]

No-one on either side foresaw that rapidly advancing trench technology and barbed wire would result in a static war of attrition quite unlike the Boer war. The cavalry had no role unless the infantry could punch a gap in the enemy front line. Both sides were on a 'learning curve'.[3] The British and the French were slow to learn that, as in urban conflict, the advantage lay with the defenders provided they had well-fortified, in-depth trench lines and adequate reserves for counter-attacks. The British tried to adapt intelligently with technical and tactical innovations in the air, on the ground and even under the ground but all of them failed to achieve a breakthrough.[4] Huge numbers of lives were lost in successive offensives in 1915 without any worthwhile gain. It had been a very bleak year.

In June 1916, Bertram wrote to Melville, 'I hear I am to go to France next week. I wish you were two years older and I would take you out with me'.[5] Mittie did not see it the same way. She wrote to him, 'I did not see Daddy off from the station but said goodbye at the hotel. You will understand more than anyone what parting with Daddy is to me and to this awful war from which so few return. We can only pray for his safety'.[6] She was concerned that if the war dragged on, Melville would be old enough to be called up and she might lose both her husband and her son.[7] When Bertram had gone, Mittie had to pack up the house at the Curragh and move the family, the ponies, the dog, the car and all their belongings back to Southington House.[8]

Bertram arrived in France on 29th June 1916, just as an artillery bombardment signaled the start of the Battle of the Somme. He wrote a daily diary. There was confusion about where he was to go but he was eventually ordered to Montreuil to command a mounted column consisting of a squadron of the 21st Lancers, two squadrons of the 2nd King Edward's Horse, about 400 cyclists and some machine gunners.[9] They were billeted just inland from Le Touquet well out of harm's way. He settled in to 'a nice little room in a very clean house. I have a sitting room downstairs which I use as an office looking out on to a pretty garden which is a mass of roses.' His 'personal servant' was Mr Fairchild from Southington.[10]

It was still assumed that if the infantry could pierce the enemy defences, the cavalry would charge through the gap into open country. Bertram's troops were therefore in reserve and were employed in repairing roads and unloading stores at the railhead. Two days after his arrival he visited the trenches at Mesnil when it was thought everything was quiet but he came under shell fire which wrecked his staff car. The driver had very sensibly taken cover in a ditch and was not hit. On July 17th Bertram made a further visit to the front at Mametz Wood, recently taken from the Germans.

It was a mass of fresh troops. Guns and lorries were being brought up along almost impassible roads being towed by caterpillar engines. Thousands of soldiers are working on the roads as the troops move forward using anything that comes in handy. Trees are cut down and broken bricks laid on top. Light railways are being built.

There were no actual exposed corpses but a number had been very hastily covered and there were legs and arms sticking out of the ground. There was a mass of debris, rifles, bayonets, ammunition, helmets, haversacks by the thousand all being collected by salvage teams. Only by visiting the ground can one realise the stupendous difficulties of attacking prepared entrenched positions. The organization of the supply department is perfectly marvelous. Every man is getting his full ration, water is laid on and thousands of horses are getting all the forage they want.[11]

On July 21st he learned that there was no prospect of a breakthrough on the Somme. For a few days his troops were moved close behind the front line. Their orders were to 'clear the battlefield'. This was a euphemism for burying the dead which had to be done at night. As the battle dragged on, his men dug trenches, constructed wired enclosures and camps for German prisoners and did anything useful behind the front line.

Bertram seems to have had a good deal of time on his hands. There was much riding round the country to lunch and dine with friends and he played polo, tennis and bridge. There were sports and steeplechases and he always went to church parade on Sundays. He received letters from home and he wrote back though he could not tell Mittie where he was because of censorship rules. Life continued in this way for the next four months and the Somme offensive eventually petered out in November.

On November 8th he received a message by telephone from his corps H.Q., 'I want to tell you that you are a General and you have been appointed to command the 7th Cavalry Brigade.' Bertram was taken entirely by surprise as he had 'never dreamed of anything of the sort'. He had done nothing noteworthy in France and the promotion was probably linked to his service in Dublin. The next day he learned that his brigade would consist of the 1st and 2nd Life Guards, the Leicester Yeomanry and the 5th Dragoons. A typical cavalry brigade consisted of about 3,000 men and a similar number of horses. As well as about 2,300 mounted cavalrymen armed with rifles there were artillerymen with their field guns, machine gunners, engineers, ambulance men, vets and headquarters staff.

Bertram's immediate response to his promotion was to take some home leave, partly to get his general's insignia in London. This included new buttons on his uniform which his daughter Moggy, aged 8, thought was a terrible waste of money, though she did demand the old ones.[12] All was well at Southington except that Charlotte had chicken pox. Nine days later he was back in France and spent his time inspecting the various regiments under his command.

During March the Germans shortened the front they had to defend by retreating to the prepared and fortified 'Hindenburg Line' from Arras southwards. Bertram occupied his time by playing golf at Le Touquet, riding in a steeplechase, watching the regimental football teams and attending lectures and concerts arranged to keep the men amused.

THE BATTLE OF ARRAS

On 29th March 1917 Bertram attended a conference of brigadiers and was shown maps of a new offensive plan which came to be called the Battle of Arras.[13]

The idea was still for the infantry to force a gap in the enemy lines and for the cavalry to charge through it into open country. On 5th April the brigade was ordered to march to Bougainville, west of Amiens.[14]

Bertram recorded in his diary,

8th April. 25-mile march to Gouy and Simoncourt. Most of the men slept under cover of some kind, horses in the open.

9th April. Divisional march order, 8th brigade, 6th brigade, 7th brigade. Urgent message to close up. Arrived at the entrance to Arras

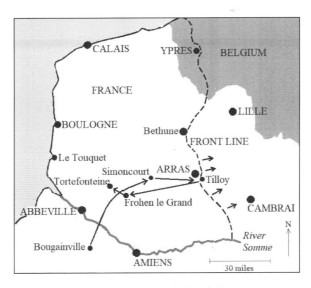

Map 11. Movements of the 7th Cavalry
Brigade, 8th – 25th April 1917.

7.30pm. Bivouacked in a field 3m west of Arras. Snowing and bitterly cold.

10th April. Moved forward to valley N of Tilloy. Slept in a trench. Intense cold and sharp frost.

11th April. Ready to move at 5am. 8th brigade moved forward. Considerable casualties from machine gun fire. 7th unable to move. 7th brigade H.Q. staff dug a hole to keep us out of the wind. Fire lit and we were having some tea. Terrific explosion followed by an avalanche of earth and stones. Crater 20ft across only 15 yards away. No-one injured.

About 3pm ordered to withdraw my brigade to the racecourse west of Arras. Snowing with no cover of any kind. Worst night I have ever experienced.

12th April. Some of the men had to be pulled out of the snow and were so cold they could not saddle their horses. Marched at 7.30am to Simoncourt.

13th April. Fine day but the mud is ankle deep. Rode round all the units.

16th April. Marched at 7.30am to Frohen le Grand. We are in a beautiful chateau and I have a room facing south.

17th April. Rode round the whole area about 18 miles. 1st and 2nd Life Guards are very badly off with no cover. No orders to move so settled to move them to Bealcourt tomorrow.

19th April. March to Tortefonteine. Watched the whole brigade march by. The area is quite good and all the horses can get under cover.

It was then quiet for the next week. Bertram rode around all his units every day and found the men contented.

Bertram was a but a small cog in a vast military machine. He obeyed his orders from day to day and sometimes from hour to hour but took no part in directing the battle and had no idea what was going on. Despite his promotion to brigadier general he was acting much as he had done as a major in the Boer War though he was commanding thirty times the numbers of troops. It was not until 25th April that he learned the outcome of the battle.[15] In the first two days spectacular advances were made. His forces were moved to the front line at Tilloy when there was hope of a breakthrough but German counter attacks forced the British back almost to where they had started. British and Imperial casualties were 158,660 dead and wounded.[16]

It had been a very hard time because of the weather but they had not engaged the enemy. Bertram had been on the Western Front for 10 months but this was the first time he had been under fire. War has long been described as 'months of boredom with moments of terror'. Since the cavalry regiments were in reserve, he and his soldiers had spent their time out of harm's way. Whilst great battles were raging, Bertram had been dining out and playing golf, polo and tennis. The infantry bore the brunt of it but they manned the trenches in rotation and had periods in reserve.[17] Bertram's experience was not unusual.

He had been able to send a telegram home on 12th April which read simply, 'All well'. Bertram would have known that Mittie would be reading the war reports in the newspapers and would be very worried. Bertram's diary ended on 25th April.

In early May he got home leave to receive his C.B. from the King, an event celebrated at home in the time-honoured fashion.[18]

Fig. 31. At Southington, May 1917.

Fig. 32. Overton, 25th April 1917. There are no men of military age in the photograph.

During this visit Bertram would have seen a painted board on the wall of Overton Post Office with the names of 230 Overton men who were serving in the army and navy which Mittie had been asked to unveil the week before. Postcards with this photograph were sent to each of the men to show they were not forgotten by the village.[19]

There were two more British offensives in 1917 but Bertram's brigade was not involved. The Battle of Passchendaele raged from July until November. At the Battle of Cambrai in November and December, massed tanks took the place of cavalry but failed to penetrate the German defences. Bertram's brigade was put in readiness just behind the front line and manned trenches for a while but was not otherwise required and they returned to their winter quarters.

The huge losses in these battles left the British defences in the Somme area weakened. Meanwhile, the Russian Revolution in October 1917 resulted in the collapse of the Eastern front, enabling the Germans to move men and materiel to reinforce their amies in France before the arrival of the Americans.

In March 1918 the 17th Lancers were added to Bertram's brigade which was one of four in the 3rd Cavalry Division.

THE GERMAN SPRING OFFENSIVE, 1918

When the expected attack came on 21st March the British defences in the area of the Somme were overwhelmed and German forces poured through the gaps into open country, pushing the British back 20-40 miles over the course of the next two weeks. It had become a war of manoeuvre in which the cavalry at last found a role because of their mobility.[20]

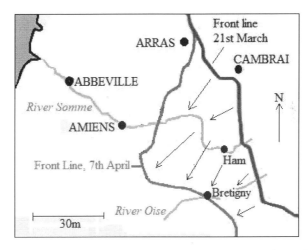

Map 12. German Spring Offensive in the Somme area, March-April 1918

The regiments of Bertram's brigade were divided into squadrons of about 200 men who were sent to reinforce the defences wherever they were needed over a very wide area, here to fill a gap, there to cover a retirement or to hold a bridge.[21] The staff work required to keep them supplied with food, water, ammunition and forage for their horses must have been immense and unremitting.

Communications were very difficult. There was no time to rig wires and poles for field telephones and they did not have radio. It was found that dispatch riders on horseback, who could gallop across fields, were quicker than motorcyclists going by roads choked with military traffic and refugees.[22]

Enemy forces crossed the Somme at Ham on March 23rd. Bertram's cavalry were sent to Villeselve to reinforce the infantry 'who were

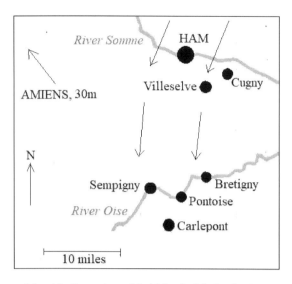

Map 13. Operations, 23rd March–5th April, 1918.

wavering'. The cavalry had several Hotchkiss light machine guns which were designed for the parts to be carried by two horses. Using them effectively, the cavalry stiffened the resistance of the infantry and rescued two battalions who were all but surrounded. In the process they killed or wounded about 100 Germans and took 100 prisoners.[23]

However, the retreat continued to a defensible line at the River Oise. The 3rd Cavalry Division H.Q. was moved from Cugny to Carlepont. Bertram, with 650 cavalrymen, was ordered to reinforce French forces between Sempigny and Bretigny who were blowing up the bridges over the river and the Oise canal.

On 1st April the 7th Cavalry Brigade was moved north-east for the defence of Amiens to the village of Gentelles, less than 10 miles from the city. On 5th April it was reported,

> The enemy attacked on the whole divisional front after an intense bombardment of 45 min. Stopped dead by machine gun and artillery fire. Enemy forming up again at about 12.45. Col. Burt reports he is strongly dug in and is confident of being able to deal with the situation. 7th Cavalry Brigade equally happy.[24]

The attack was repulsed. By April 7th the whole front line was stabilised and the German offensive had petered out.

The same day Bertram received a letter from the Officer Commanding the 9th Australian Infantry Brigade.

> May I take the opportunity of expressing my keen appreciation of the prompt and most valuable assistance rendered to my troops on the left flank by your Royal Dragoons and 17th Lancers. As has happened so often in the recent fighting, the cavalry on the morning of 4th April undoubtedly saved the situation. Charles Rosenthal, Major General, 7th April 1918.[25]

The 7th Cavalry Brigade was brought together again but got no rest. On 10th April another German attack was made to the north and they were sent there. However, on this occasion the front line was not breached and they retired to St Pol. The Germans had failed to take the railhead at Amiens on which the British front in the Somme area depended.

On 17th April Bertram's place as commander of the 7th Cavalry Brigade was taken by another and he returned home.[26] By this time there was no shortage of younger officers well qualified for promotion to this level. It seems to have been at his own request since he had served continuously as a Reserve Officer for nearly four years. Family letters indicate that he was planning to leave but delayed his departure until the expected German offensive was over.[27] He had done his duty and was allowed to retire. There was a conference involving the brigadier generals commanding the cavalry brigades on 13th April to review the recent engagements and this may well have been when the decision was made.[28]

Meanwhile, the alarming reports of the German offensive had caused wild rumours to circulate in Overton. Mittie wrote,

> Last night Louisa came in with a white face and said all the village is out saying Paris has fallen and the war will be decided in 24hrs. ... I sent Mr Ward tearing up to Laverstoke to find nothing of the sort had

happened. He was furious and would have gone into the street and fought the man who spread the report but we have not found out who started it.[29]

There were more alarms to come but by early summer, with the failure of the German Spring Offensive, reinforcements from England and the eventual arrival of the Americans in numbers, the outcome of the war was no longer in serious doubt.

In March 1918 Mittie referred to the Germans as 'those hordes with their devilish tricks'.[30] In his diary and letters from France, Bertram never revealed what he thought about the Germans or the conduct of the war. This is in contrast with his diaries of the Boer War in which he seemed to have a sneaking admiration for 'brother Boer' and roundly criticized the British generals. He may have been mindful of the censors. In his letters from France he never revealed where he was. He may also have been careful about what he wrote in his diary in case both he and the diary should fall into enemy hands. What he wrote about was obeying orders, doing his duty and the welfare of his men and their horses.

Shortly after he arrived home, Bertram spoke to the children at Overton School on 24th May, Empire Day, about the meaning of Empire and the duty of patriotism.[31]

CHAPTER 9:

A LONG RETIREMENT, 1918-1949

When Bertram came home he found that much had changed. There was great sadness in the family. Two of his brother Spencer's sons and his sister Eveline's son had been killed in the war and both of his brother William's daughters had lost their husbands. Overton had lost 34 men.

By 1918 ration cards had been introduced and even the gentry were affected by shortages. Nan Jagg wrote to Melville, 'We are not starving. We manage to feed on something, chiefly vegetables. We had butter for a week but now there is none. The children get an egg once a week'.[1]

Charlotte, 14, wrote, 'We do nothing here but lessons and sawing wood. We have to supply the schoolroom as we are not allowed any coal'.[2] The world of Bertram's youth had gone.

Spanish flu was also affecting the village. Moggy Portal, aged 10, wrote,

> There is quite a lot of people who have got the flew here and about four have died of it. Mrs Titmous has got it now so there was no-one to play the organ for church this morning. All five of us went. Hytie and I did not go to Sunday School because there is so much flew about.[3]

Charlotte wrote on the same day that she had been to her first 'grown-up' dance the night before.[4] The disease was well known to be highly infectious and fatalities were widely reported in the newspapers, the risk being greatest in young adults. It was thought wise not to let the children go to Sunday school but dances and church services continued as usual. What we now call 'social distancing' was not applied.

When news of the Armistice reached Overton, Bertram wrote to Melville,

> The wonderful news came yesterday. I was at the mill with Uncle Willie and we had a notice put up and the flag hoisted at 12 o'clock and all the workers cheered lustily as they came out. The church bells rang at Overton and we had a special service at 7.30 to which everyone in the house went including your five sisters. The church was packed and it was a really impressive service. I distributed champagne all round.[5]

Bertram was then 52. Once again he devoted his energies to village affairs. When the peace treaty was eventually signed at Versailles in 1919, he hosted a great celebration over two evenings in the grounds of Southington House with sports, a bonfire and dancing. He also revived the Boy Scouts and chaired the War Memorial Committee.[6]

Money for the memorial was raised by public subscription but there was great debate in the village about what form it should take. Some favoured a stone cross but others wanted a lych gate. After heated discussions, Bertram had to resort to a referendum to decide the issue. A stone cross was erected.[7]

In his father's day there had been almost feudal deference to the gentry and clergy. Issues of this sort would have been decided by them in a world where people 'knew their place'. The gentry would also have paid for it. In the post-war world the people had found their voice. Having subscribed to the fund they expected to have their say on how the money was spent.

It was intended that the money remaining in the memorial fund should be used to rebuild the Working Men's Club on a new site.[8]

Fig. 33. Overton Memorial Institute in 2019.

Before the war it had been run by the rector and William Portal as a means of keeping 'the labouring classes' out of the pubs. There were lectures and a library to 'improve their minds'. As a dry club, closed on Sundays, it did not flourish and was only kept going by subscriptions from the gentry.[9]

A new site was acquired from the Portal family for £1 but more fundraising was needed to achieve this object. When the new club was eventually opened in 1923 it was called the 'Overton Imperial Memorial Institute' in commemoration of those killed in the war and it was linked to the British Legion. The new building had a bar. At the gala opening the Rector addressed the assembled company, urging them to continue the lectures, but his words fell on deaf ears.[10] The members were quite clear that they had no desire for total abstinence and were not going to be told by the clergy and gentry to 'improve their minds'. Bertram was appointed chair of the 'Stute' committee and it became a very successful social club. He was well respected in the village but it was not automatic. He earned respect for what he did.

Even before the war ended, Bertram joined a small group of prominent Hampshire people who took the initiative to create Enham

Village near Andover for the medical treatment and training of ex-servicemen suffering from the effects of amputations and shell shock.[11] It provided the model for several such villages eventually funded by King George V and the Red Cross. The men were retrained in trades such as basketry, upholstery, market gardening, boot repairs, electrical fitting and poultry farming.[12] Existing buildings were enough to accommodate 150 men, and the first 50 injured soldiers arrived in the summer of 1919. By the end of 1921, 510 men had been admitted to Enham and 366 had been discharged, 80% of whom were able to take up employment or industrial training.[13] At a fundraising garden fete at Enham Village in July 1920, 'the Hon. Mrs B. Portal arranged a play performed by local schoolchildren'.[14] Her daughters performed in the entertainment as well.[15]

By 1920 Bertram had been elected to the Parochial Church Council and was chair of the Parish Council and the Recreation Committee.[16] He was closely involved with everything that happened in the village. By 1926 he had added the Horticultural Society and the Overton Choral Society to his list of chairmanships.[17] The whole family were involved, this report being but one example.

> On Wednesday evening last, a social was held in St Mary's Hall in aid of the local boy scouts and wolf cubs. Under the energetic leadership of Miss Charlotte Portal and Miss Hyacinthe Portal a useful band of young wolf cubs is being formed. The Misses Portal gave instrumental pieces on the violin and cello and the Hon. Mrs B. Portal and Mrs F. Titmous shared the accompanying throughout the evening.[18]

As before, the grounds of Southington House were in regular use for fundraising events and the five daughters continued to perform in plays and concerts on many occasions.

Bertram returned to work at the family paper business. In 1920 it became a private company with William Wyndham as chairman with Bertram, his brother Spencer and Wyndham Raymond Portal, William's son, as directors.[19] Bertram's remuneration as an 'ordinary' director was

Fig. 34. The five sisters in costume for a performance of Robin Hood, 1923.

fixed at one twentieth of the net profits but not less than £500. This was much less than the other 'executive' directors. Though he attended board meetings regularly there is nothing in the company records to show what contribution he made.[20]

Sometime after the war, Bertram built Dellands House, close to Southington House, for his daughters to live in if they did not marry. In the event, none of them ever lived there. Bertram let it to an army colleague, Major Gordon Dill, who he had introduced to the Mill after the war and who became an executive director in 1922.[21]

Melville became engaged in 1926. He had followed rather precisely in his father's footsteps being trained at Sandhurst, serving in an Indian garrison in the 17th Lancers and then as A.D.C. to the Governor of Madras, Viscount Goschen. He then became engaged to the Governor's daughter Cicely.

His parents did not go to the wedding but their daughter Charlotte went as a bridesmaid.[22] It was a sumptuous occasion and Charlotte fell in love with the Governor's new A.D.C. They were married in Overton in 1929.[23] Later the same year, Hytie was married in Shanghai.[24] In 1937

Fig. 35. Melville's wedding in Madras, 1926.

Bertram's youngest daughter Cecilia was married in Overton to Nigel Hoare and Moggy was married in Overton in 1939.[25]

As time went by Bertram's interests broadened to encompass the County of Hampshire. He resumed his support for the Hampshire Territorial Association and in 1925 became chairman and had considerable success in boosting recruitment. It was for this service that he was created K.C.B. in 1937, a knighthood being his highest honour.[26] He was treasurer of the Hampshire Boy Scouts Association and in 1932 was elected to the Hampshire County Council. Bertram was appalled by the toll of road accidents and used his position to campaign for improved safety on the roads. In November 1940 he brought to the Council's attention that in six months there had been 90 fatal accidents in Hampshire, 44 of which involved military vehicles.[27] He became Deputy Lieutenant of Hampshire in 1932 and a county alderman in 1943. These were largely ceremonial posts but they reflected the contribution he had made to the county. He was particularly proud to be appointed a Governor of Wellington College, where he had been educated, in 1934. In 1937 he took on the duties of churchwarden at St Mary's Church in Overton.[28]

BERTRAM PORTAL-MARGARET LITTLETON

Melville m Cicely Goschen Simon d. 2021 ———— Simon d. 2021

Charlotte m James LongfieldDesmond ———— Desmond
Susan d. 1970

Hyacinthe m Malcolm Mackintosh ———— Angus
Anne

Margaret m John Litchfield ———— Mark
Sophie d.1992
Virginia

Sophie

Cecilia m Nigel Hoare ———— Hyacinthe
Joanna
Louisa
Henrietta d. 1969

Bertram's children and grandchildren.

At the outbreak of war in 1939, Cecilia and her husband and their little daughter came to live at Southington House for much of the time. Bertram was then 73 and was suffering considerably from arthritis. He visited Bath from time to time to 'take the waters' in the belief this might relieve his pain. One night in April 1942 he was at the Francis Hotel in the city when the air-raid sirens sounded. The hotel rule was that all guests should take to the cellars until the 'all-clear' was sounded but Bertram, by then tucked up in his warm bed, did not fancy the idea at all and stayed firmly where he was.

Next day the room porter asked how he found it down below and was horrified to hear the truth. He said he would lose his job if guests on his floor did not comply with the rules. The next night the sirens sounded again. Bertram, not wishing to cause any more bother, got out of bed and went down to the cellar with the other guests. On returning to his room he found a large hole where his bed had been. A bomb had gone through the ceiling and down to the floor below where it lodged without exploding.[29] Later that night there was a further alarm and a 500kg bomb destroyed most of the hotel.[30] Two firewatchers were killed but everyone in the basement survived.[31]

Fig 36. The Francis Hotel Bath, April 1942.

By this time Bertram was shedding some of his responsibilities but continued as chairman of the Overton Institute and as churchwarden. In 1943 he chaired the Overton and Whitchurch 'Wings for Victory' campaign, better known as the 'Spitfire Fund', to encourage local people to buy government bonds in support of the war effort. It raised £65,000, enough to build 13 planes.[32]

Joanna, Cecilia's second daughter, remembers her grandfather in old age.

He was a very gentle and gentlemanly old man. We never dreamt of being rude or shouting or arguing in his presence. He was a very meticulous man with a love of order and routine but, although he did not show emotion, he had a twinkling side to him. Because the dining room floor was not level, he led a game of rolling our napkin rings down the table. He used to read to me and my sister every day after tea and it was always the same ritual. He read the index in our book of stories. We said 'stop' when he reached the one we wanted. He also made up all sorts of little rhymes for us, some of which I remember to this day.

He was very proud of his garden though not a gardener in the modern sense of the word. He took great delight in walking with us around the garden. I remember us planting a chestnut tree which was exactly the height of my sister and we used to go and measure it to see how it was growing. It is now an enormous, splendid tree.

My grandfather never learned to drive. He tried but, being a cavalryman, could only pull on the steering wheel and say 'Whoa' when he wanted to stop!

On Sundays we always attended Matins *en famille* and usually took what we called the 'church walk', across the river and inside the wall up to a gate on Silk Mill Lane. Because of his bad knee he always used a stick and liked to have his other hand on my shoulder. I remember sitting on his knee through some of the longer sermons.

In December 1943 Bertram and Mittie learned that their son Melville was a prisoner of war, held by the Japanese at the notorious Changi Prison, Singapore.[33] They had no further news of him.

*Fig. 37. Bertram with grandchildren, 1939. They were
Moggy's children, Mark, Sophie and Virginia Litchfield.*

On 26th January 1945 Bertram, Mittie and Cecilia drove to Winchester and had an accident. The *Hampshire Chronicle* reported that the car skidded on a bridge near the cattle market and Mittie

Fig. 38. Margaret, Lady Portal.

was injured.[34] This was not the whole story. A son-in-law wrote in his diary, 'Appalling accident last Friday, when the General, Lady Portal and Cecilia were motoring to Winchester and collided with an American army lorry. The General badly bruised, Mama 3 ribs and a bone in her back broken, and Cecilia badly hurt with her baby only 3 weeks to go'.[35]

Mr Kemp, Bertram's butler, was driving and was entirely exonerated.[36] Why did the

Hampshire Chronicle not mention the American army lorry? It is ironic that Bertram's family had suffered in this way when he had campaigned so hard to reduce accidents involving military vehicles.

Mittie was taken to a nursing home where she was recovering well but had a sudden heart attack and died 12 days later.[37] After her funeral the Rector of Overton spoke of the contrast between service performed as a duty and spontaneous acts of love.

> Therein lay the secret of the affection and respect the people of Overton felt for Lady Portal. She had learnt the art of loving in the home. For more than 40 years she had been the first lady in the parish and she had set out a true example of the Christian way of life. She had not cared for her home nor come to church because it was her duty. She had just loved and delighted in her children and grandchildren; she worshipped God because she loved to do it and from her home that spirit spread outwards. Only last summer we all enjoyed the hospitality of her house and garden and she was always available for parish activities.

The same could have been said about Bertram too. They had been married for 45 years and this was a devasting blow. He was consoled by his daughters and the presence of grandchildren but still did not know whether Melville was alive or dead. It was not until September that he was known to be safe and he returned home in October.[38]

By the time the war ended, Cecilia and her family were living permanently at Southington House. The faithful, long-serving Mr Kemp catered for Bertram's

Fig. 39. Bertram in 1944.

every need. He shaved him every morning with much stropping of the cut-throat razor. He helped Bertram to dress, answered the door, served at table and organised the household.

On Sunday 4th February 1949 Bertram went to church as usual and placed some flowers on Mittie's grave. In the afternoon he counted the crocuses in his garden and played with his grandchildren before they went to bed. That night he died on his sleep.[39] He was 83.

A lengthy obituary in the *Hampshire Chronicle* listed his military achievements and honours as well as his contributions to village and Hampshire affairs. At the end, an Overton correspondent wrote,

> Sir Bertram will be much missed for he led the village life in all its activities. His genial and kindly disposition endeared him to everyone and gave him the valued ability to smooth over any difficulties. His personal touch was most marked for he was no figurehead. … Keenly interested in youth, he aided football and to the end had his chair brought out to enable him to watch the weekly football matches of the newly formed Youth Club who play immediately in front of his house at Southington.
>
> Through all he did there ran the same quiet and unwavering integrity of faith, character and purpose and the same devotion to the service of God and his fellow men.
>
> No-one can think of Sir Bertram without thinking also of his home at Southington where he, Lady Portal and their family radiated their own atmosphere of love and happiness to their friends and neighbours. It all seems so complete. May he rest in peace.[40]

POSTSCRIPT

His obituary sounds too good to be true as obituaries often are. And yet it was all true. In all my researches I did not find any flaws of character to explore. He did not go after other women, he did not have a drink problem, there were no scandals or great personal conflicts. With no skeletons in his cupboard, it could be said that Bertram Portal is a rather boring subject for a biography. He did not rise from rags to riches. He had all the advantages of his family's wealth and connections. Nor did he suffer an unhappy childhood. He was not hugely ambitious and did not achieve national prominence. Had he stayed in the army in 1907 he might, like his friend Douglas Haig, have been amongst the most senior commanders in 1914. He decided to put his family first and would have been content to live out his life as a country gentleman had a world war not intervened.

Despite his having led an apparently blameless life, writing his biography has not been boring at all. He was not a Cromwell or a Haig or a Montgomery but I could identify with him. I liked him. I wish I could have known him.

As the youngest son, Bertram had to make his own way in life. He did not choose to be a soldier. That decision was effectively made by his father by sending him to Wellington College. When Bertram was a young officer, the army valued 'character' more highly than brains which led to the stereotypical image of the British officer being pompous, jingoistic and not very bright.[1] Bertram was none of these. He was not a 'high flyer' at Sandhurst but it is quite clear from his diaries that as an officer he had both 'character' and a good brain which he used effectively. He was observant, thoughtful and decisive. It is also clear that the welfare of his soldiers and their horses was always to the fore, both as a garrison commander in peacetime and when in action. He was a true gentleman – honourable, courteous, considerate to all and modest about his achievements. He was steady, methodical and capable with a strong sense of duty, guided throughout his life by his Christian faith.

Bertram seemed to enjoy everything he did especially his sporting activities. We may not approve of him killing wild animals for fun but no-one at the time would have questioned it. We may not approve of his attitude towards the education of Indians but it was a view shared by almost every Englishman of his generation. He was a man of his time.

After the First World War he did not rest on his laurels. He had commanded thousands of men but it was not beneath his dignity as chair of the parish council to sort out the problems with the parish pump. He was still ready to serve. In 1937 he took on the duties of a churchwarden at St Mary's Overton when he was seventy-one. He was still a churchwarden when he died 12 years later. His obituary was absolutely right.

LIST OF ILLUSTRATIONS

CHAPTER 1: EARLY LIFE

CHAPTER 2: YOUNG OFFICER.

CHAPTER 3: COURTSHIP AND MARRIAGE.

CHAPTER 4: BOER WAR

Fig. 12. Bertram's spare horse carrying his kit and its own forage, by kind permission of the family.

Fig. 13. The regiment parading in the snow just prior to their departure for South Africa, Feb. 1900. National Army Museum, 1975-01-40.

Fig. 14. Capt. B. P. Portal outside his tent at Bloemfontein before departure, by kind permission of the family.

Fig. 15. Telegram, 7th Jun. 1900, by kind permission of the family.

Fig. 16. British blockhouse, National Army Museum, NAM, 1971-01-35-82.

CHAPTER 5: COLONEL OF THE REGIMENT

Fig. 17. 17th Lancers polo team at the Hurlingham Club, by kind permission of the family.

Fig. 18. Bertram in 1904, by kind permission of the family.

Fig. 19. Bertram's stud at Meerut, National Army Museum, 1975-01-40.

Fig. 20. Inspection by the Viceroy of India at Agra, January 1907, National Army Museum, 1975-01-40.

CHAPTER 6: A COUNTRY GENTLEMAN

Fig. 21. Southington House from the east in 2021. Author's photogragh.

Fig. 22. Bertram and Lord Hatherton with fishing gear and Mittie with the children, Southington House, c1908, by kind permission of the family.

Fig. 23. Programme for a Fete at Southington House, 1909, by kind permission of Jim Stickland.

Fig. 24. Overton Scouts at Atherfield Chine, 1909, by kind permission of Overton Pictures.

CHAPTER 7: IRELAND AND THE EASTER RISING IN DUBLIN

Fig. 25. Bertram with Melville, Charlotte and Hyacinthe at Curragh camp, by kind permission of the family.

LIST OF MAPS

All the maps were drawn by the author from published information.

REFERENCES

HRO is the Hampshire Record Office (Hampshire Archives). *ODNB* is the Oxford Dictionary of National Biography. TNA is The National Archives, Kew.

CHAPTER 1: EARLY LIFE

1   Census, 1871.
2   Census, 1881.
3   Sir Francis Portal, *Portals* (Oxford, 1962), 20.
4   Ibid, 29.
5   Overton Tithe Apportionment, 1847, HRO, 21M65/F7/181/1.
6   J. Bateman, *The Great Landowners of Great Britain and Ireland,* 4th ed., revised, (London, 1883), 363.
7   *ODNB*, Melville Portal.
8   Sir Francis Portal, *Portals* (Oxford, 1962), 72-5.
9   Obituary, *Hampshire Advertiser*, 23 Sept. 1905.
10   Obituary, *The Times*, 16 Sept. 1905.
11   R. Waldram *et al*, *A History of Overton from 1500* (Heritage Overton, 2019), 66, 97, 118, 122.
12   Rules of the Overton Reading Society, 1853, unpublished document held by Richard Oram, Overton.
13   Overton National School Accounts, 1844, unpublished document held by Richard Oram, Overton.
14   W. S. Portal, The poor and how to help them, HRO, 39M89/G7.
15   Memoranda of the Overton Working Men's Club, 1871, unpublished

document held by Richard Oram, Overton. The Working Men's Club was succeeded by Overton Institute, see Chapter 9.

16   Rules of Overton Cricket Club, 1851; Overton National School, 1851, unpublished documents held by Richard Oram, Overton.

17   *Hants & Berks Gazette*, 24 Jan. 1880.

18   Letter to Bertram from his parents in Austria, 1873, Bertram Portal, miscellaneous papers, 1866-1910, HRO, 6A08/E2.

19   B.P. Portal, 'A Link with the Past', unpublished manuscript, by kind permission of the family.

20   To remember the Sabbath Day and keep it holy.

21   The turnpike road was the route from London to Exeter via Basingstoke and Andover.

22   The vault was in a chapel, since demolished, in the grounds of Laverstoke House.

23   Including the Overton Working Men's Club. Memoranda of the Overton Working Men's Club, 1871, unpublished document held by Richard Oram, Overton.

24   *The Wellingtonian*, 7-8, (1881-3), Wellington College Archives.

25   Sandhurst Archives, https://sandhurstcollection.co.uk/people/3888570-cadet-bertram-portal-register-entry. (Accessed 12 Feb. 2021.)

26   A.F. Mockler Ferryman, *Annals of Sandhurst* (London, 1900), 67.

27   Ibid, 303.

28   W. S. Churchill, *My Early Life* (London, 1947), 43.

29   Ibid.

30   Sandhurst Archives, https://sandhurstcollection.co.uk/people/3888570-cadet-bertram-portal-register-entry. (Accessed 12 Feb. 2021.)

CHAPTER 2: YOUNG OFFICER

1   Bertram Portal, Service Record, TNA, WO 76/11.

2   British military sites in India. https://usacac.army.mil/sites/default/files/documents/carl/nafziger/887EAF.pdf. (Accessed 12 Feb. 2021)

3   W.S. Churchill, *My Early Life* (London, 1947), 103-6.

4   *Field*, 6 Aug. 1887.

5   *Hampshire Chronicle*, 16 Oct. 1886.

6   *Canterbury Journal, Kentish Times and Farmers' Gazette*, 24 Apr. 1889.

7   Letter from Bertram to his mother, 8 Aug. 1889, by kind permission of the family.

8   *Army and Navy Gazette*, 25 Oct. 1890; Bertram Portal, service record, TNA, WO 76/11;

9   *Army and Navy Gazette*, 25 Jun. 1892; Ibid, 23 Feb. 1895.

10   J.W. Fortescue, *A History of the 17th Lancers* (London, 1895), 179.

11   *Field*, 15 Jun. 1895; *Leeds Mercury*, 23 Apr. 1895; *Grantham Journal*, 4 Jan. 1896.

12   *Army and Navy Gazette*, 22 Feb. 1896.

13   *Homeward Mail from India, China and the East*, 4 Apr. 1896.

14   Letter from Bertram to his mother, 25 May1896, British Library, Mss Eur F494.

15   W. S. Churchill, *My Early Life* (London, 1947), 154.

16   Letter from Bertram to his mother, 11 May 1898, British Library, Mss Eur F494.

17   Ibid, 15 Apr. 1896.

18   *Englishman's Overland Mail*, 31 Mar. 1898.

19   *Homeward Mail from India, China and the East*, 4 Jun. 1898.

20   Letter from Bertram to his mother, 25 May 1897, British Library, Mss Eur F494.

21   Ibid.

22   Ibid.

23   Letter from Bertram to Spencer, 6 Apr. 1898, HRO, 6A08/E2.

24   *Homeward Mail from India, China and the East*, 17 Dec. 1898. The scheduled date for arrival in London was 23 Dec.

CHAPTER 3: COURTSHIP AND MARRIAGE

1   *Staffordshire Advertiser*, 15 Apr. 1899.

2   *Hampshire Advertiser*, 13 Jun. 1888.

3   A. Tinniswood, B*ehind the Throne: a Domestic History of the Royal Family* (London, 2018), 238-40.

4   M. Allingham, Marriage in British India, https://merrynallingham. com/19th-20th-century/marriage-in-british-india. (Accessed 3 Mar. 2021.)

5   *Daily Telegraph & Courier (London)*, 10 May 1890.

6   Littleton family, estate papers, Staffordshire Archives, D5378.

7   *Morning Post*, 15 May 1899.

8   Census, 1881.

9   B.P. Portal, A Link with the Past, unpublished manuscript, by kind permission of the family.

10   Service Record, TNA, WO 76/11.

11   Mittie's autograph book, by kind permission of the family.

12   *Staffordshire Advertiser*, 10 Nov. 1894.

13   *Reading Mercury*, 29 Dec. 1894.

14   *Cannock Chase Courier*, 10 Dec. 1898; *Sheffield Daily Telegraph*, 16 Apr. 1898.

15   They had served together in the regiment as lieutenants, 1886-92. J.W. Fortescue, *A History of the 17th Lancers* (Macmillan, 1895), Appendix A.

16   *North Down Herald and County Down Independent*, 17 Feb. 1899.

17   *The Times*, 18 Feb. 1899.

18   *Staffordshire Advertiser*, 15 Apr. 1899.

19   Recollections of Constance Portal, unpublished manuscript, by kind permission of the family.

20   Marriage Settlement, Staffordshire Archives, D260/M/T/6/118.

21   Census, Ireland, 1901.

22   Recollections of Constance Portal, unpublished manuscript, by kind permission of the family.

CHAPTER 4: BOER WAR

1   Bertram Portal, miscellaneous papers, 1866-1910, HRO, 6A08/E2.

2   *Daily Telegraph & Courier* (London), 13 Jan. 1900

3   *E.g. Morning Post*, 8 Jun. 1900.

4   *British Medical Journal*, 2 Feb. 1901.

5   The diaries of Maj. Bertram Percy Portal, covering service with the 17th

Lancers in the Boer War, Feb. to Sept. 1900, National Army Museum, 2008-07-17.

6   *London Evening Standard*, 15 Feb. 1900.

7   The diaries of Maj. Bertram Percy Portal covering service with the 17th Lancers in the Boer War, Feb. to Sept. 1900, National Army Museum, 2008-07-17.

8   G. Micholls, *A History of the 17th Lancers, 1895-1923* (London, 1931), 21.

9   Letter from Bertram to Mittie, 19 Mar. 1900 by kind permission of the family.

10   W. S. Churchill, *My Early Life* (London, 1947), 329.

11   Constance Portal, *Recollections of Malshanger,* by kind permission of the family

12. Letter from Bertram to Mittie, 2 May 1900, by kind permission of the family.

13. G. Micholls, *A History of the 17th Lancers*, 1895-1923 (London, 1931), 27.

14. The diaries of Maj. Bertram Percy Portal covering service with the 17th Lancers in the Boer War, Feb. to Sept. 1900, National Army Museum, 2008-07-17.

15. W. S. Churchill, *Ian Hamilton's March* (London, 1900), 174.

16. The diaries of Maj. Bertram Percy Portal covering service with the 17th Lancers in the Boer War, Feb. to Sept. 1900, National Army Museum, 2008-07-17.

17. Mittie gave birth to a son at 55 Warwick Square, the Littleton family's town house in London, on 1 Jun, Morning Post, 6 Jun. 1900.

18. Letter from Bertram to Mittie, 8 Jun. 1900, by kind permission of the family.

19. Ibid, 27 Jun. 1900.

20. *Hants & Berks Gazette*, 15 Sept. 1900.

21. *Hampshire Chronicle*, 22 Sept. 1900.

22. Census, Ireland, Mar.1901.

23. Bertram's Diary, Aug. 1901 to Jun. 1902, unpublished manuscript, by kind permission of the family.

24. Ibid.

25. A kloof is a steep-sided, wooded ravine.

26. Bertram's Diary, Aug. 1901 to Jun. 1902, unpublished manuscript, by kind permission of the family.

27. Letter from Bertram to Spencer, 8 Dec. 1901, HRO, 6A08/E2.

28. Diary of Margaret Portal (Mittie) in Capetown, HRO, 6A08/F3.

29. Ibid.

30. *The Scotsman*, 2 Oct. 1902.

31. *The London Gazette*, 29 Jul. 1902, 4839.

CHAPTER 5: COLONEL OF THE REGIMENT

1   *Edinburgh Evening News*, 20 Oct. 1902.

2   G. Micholls, *A History of the 17th Lancers, 1895-1923* (London, 1931), 57.

3   Bertram Portal, miscellaneous papers, 1866-1910, HRO, 5M52/T58.

4   *Army & Navy Gazette,* 6 Feb. 1904.

5   *Portsmouth Evening News*, 10 Nov. 1903.

6   G. Micholls, *A History of the 17th Lancers, 1895-1923* (London, 1931), 57.

7   *Army & Navy Gazette*, 1 Jul. 1905.

8   *Dundee Evening Telegraph*, 20 Jun. 1905.

9   *Army & Navy Gazette*, 1 Jul. 1905.

10 *Aberdeen Press and Journal*, 11 Aug. 1903.

11 Baden Powell was not well thought of by the army commanders in South Africa because they maintained that he should never have allowed his superior forces to be surrounded by the Boers at Mafeking. He was made Inspector of the Cape Police to ensure that he would not command of men in the field again. He was later became Inspector of Cavalry, Home Forces.

12 *Edinburgh Evening News*, 3 May 1904.

13 Letter from Col. Portal to Robert Baden Powell, 21 Nov. 1904, HRO, 6A08/E3.

14 *Bailey's Magazine*, 28 Aug. 1903.

15 *E.g. Yorkshire Post and Leeds Intelligencer*, 12 Dec. 1903.

16 *Edinburgh Evening News*, 1 Jul. 1904; *Berwick Advertiser*, 8 Apr. 1904.

17 *Northern Chronicle and General Advertiser for the North of Scotland*, 11 Sept. 1907.

18 *London Evening Standard*, 13 May 1903.

19 *The Scotsman*, 8 May 1905; Ibid, 26 May 1903; Ibid, 2 Dec. 1904.

20 *Edinburgh Evening News*, 10 Sept. 1904.

21 *Edinburgh Evening News*, 15 Jul. 1905.

22 *Daily Telegraph & Courier (London),* 11 Jul. 1905.

23 Long-serving non-commissioned officers were allowed to marry. Their wives and children were 'on the regiment' and had to be transported and housed wherever the regiment went.

24 *Edinburgh Evening News*, 6 Sept. 1905.

25 *Morning Post*, 8 Sept. 1905.

26 Sir Francis Portal*, Portals,* (Oxford, 1962), 89.

27 H. R. Nevill, *Meerut Gazetteer* (Allalabad, 1904), 4, 275.

28 Letter from Mittie to her mother, 10 Oct. 1905, by kind permission of the family.

29 G. Micholls, *A History of the 17th Lancers, 1895-1923* (London, 1931), 62.

30 *Army & Navy Gazette*, 2 Nov. 1907.

31 Ibid, 28 Dec. 1907.

32 G. Micholls, *A History of the 17th Lancers, 1895-1923* (London, 1931), 81.

33 *Field*, 31 Mar. 1906; *The Sportsman*, 4 May 1906.

34 G. Micholls, *A History of the 17th Lancers, 1895-1923* (London, 1931), 74.

35 Letter from Mittie to her mother, 28 Mar. 1906, by kind permission of the family.

36 Letter from Mittie to Melville, 7 Mar. 1906, HRO, 6A08/J3.

37 Letter from Mittie to Melville, 11 Jan. 1906, HRO, 6A08/J3.

38 *The Sportsman*, 5 Apr. 1906.

39 Letter from Bertram to Melville, 14 Dec. 1905, HRO, 6A08/J3.

40 Letter from Douglas Haig to Bertram, 28 Feb. 1906, HRO, 6A08/E3.

41 Letters from Bertram to Melville, 17 May 1906 and 18 Oct. 1906, HRO, 6A08/J3.

42 Letter from Bertram to Melville, 3 Jan. 1907, HRO, 6A08/J3.

43 Letter from Douglas Haig to Bertram, 6 Oct. 1906, HRO 6A08/E3.

44 *Army & Navy Gazette*, 23 Nov. 1907.

45 Hansard, https://api.parliament.uk/historic-hansard/commons/1907/mar/14/army-estimates-1907-8. (Accessed 2 Feb 2021.)

46 *Army & Navy Gazette*, 16 Nov. 1907.

47 Ibid, 4 May 1907.

48 Letters from Bertram to Melville, 4 Apr. 1907 and 21 Apr. 1907, HRO, 6A08/J3.

49 *Army & Navy Gazette*, 1 Jun. 1907.

CHAPTER 6: A COUNTRY GENTLEMAN

1   *Homeward Mail from India, China and the East*, 25 May 1907; Census, England, 1901.

2   Plan of Southington House and lands in Overton, *c*.1900, HRO, 10M57/P143/1.

3   Census, England, 1911.

4   Letter from Bertram to Melville addressed to the school, 24 Jul. 1913, HRO, 6A08/E4.

5   Census, England, 1911.

6   Census, Ireland, 1901.

7   *Hants & Berks Gazette*, 24 Aug. 1907.

8   Sir Francis Portal, *Portals* (Oxford, 1962), 89.

9   Contract of employment, Bertram Portal, miscellaneous Papers, 1910-1940, HRO, 6A08/E4.

10 Correspondence with W. B. Peat and Co., 1908-1909, HRO, 132M98/A3/2.

11 *Hampshire Chronicle*, 13 Nov. 1909.

12 Ibid, 4 Apr. 1908; Ibid, 9 May 1909.

13 *Hampshire Chronicle*, 12 Apr. 1907.

14 Ibid, 13 Feb. 1910.

15 *Hants and Berks Gazette*, 5 Oct. 1907.

16 Ibid, 16 Apr. 1910.

17 Overton Parish Council minute book, HRO, 27M80/PX2.

18 *Hants & Berks Gazette*, 3 Aug. 1907; Ibid 10 Aug. 1907; *Hampshire Chronicle,* 28 Nov. 1908.

19 *Hants & Berks Gazette*, 28 Sept. 1907; Ibid, 23 Apr. 1910.

20 Census, 1911.

21 Ann Pitcher, *A History of Overton* (Author, 1984), 49. Her principal informant was Cecilia Hoare, Bertram's youngest daughter.

22 *Hampshire Chronicle,* 21 Aug. 1909.

23 Ibid.

24 *Hants &Berks Gazette*, 17 Dec. 1910.

25 Ibid, 28 Jan. 1911.

26 Secret communication from the War Office, 13 Mar. 1914, Bertram Portal, miscellaneous Papers, 1910-1940, HRO, 6A08/E4.

27 *Hants & Berks Gazette,* 26 Aug. 1914.

CHAPTER 7: IRELAND AND THE EASTER RISING IN DUBLIN

1   Bertram Portal, miscellaneous papers, 1910-1940, HRO, 6A08/E4.

2   Proceedings of a Court of Enquiry on the Administration of the Army Remount Department since January 1899 (HMSO, London, 1922), 396.

3   Bertram Portal, miscellaneous papers, 1910-1940, HRO, 6A08/E4.

4   Reserve Regiments of Cavalry, https://www.longlongtrail.co.uk/army/regiments-and-corps/cavalry-regiments/the-reserve-regiments-of-cavalry. (Accessed 18 Feb. 2021.)

5   Letter from Bertram to Melville, 16 Oct. 1914, HRO, 6A08/J2.

6   Ibid, 1 Nov. 1914, HRO, 6A08/J2.

7   Ibid, 17 Mar. 1916, HRO, 6A08/J2.

8   Ibid, 1 Nov. 1914. HRO, 6A08/J2.

9   G. Micholls, *A History of the 17th Lancers, 1895-1923* (London, 1931), 84.

10 R. Grayson, *Dublin's Great Wars: The First World War, the Easter Rising and the Irish Revolution* (Cambridge, 2018), 45-6.

11 Letter from Bertram to Melville, 1 Nov. 1914, HRO, 6A08/J2.

12 Letter from H. Gough to Bertram, 18 Dec. 1914, HRO, 6A08/E4.

13 The Suspensory Act, 18 Sept. 1914.

14 R. Grayson, *Dublin's Great Wars: The First World War, the Easter Rising and the Irish Revolution* (Cambridge, 2018), 362.

15 Intelligence report on the state of Ireland from Headquarters, Irish Command, 10 Apr. 1916, University College Dublin Archives, https://doi.org/10.7925/drs1.ucdlib_53988. (Accessed 18 Feb. 2021.)

16 Report of the Royal Commission on the Rebellion in Ireland, Minutes of Evidence (HMSO,1916), 54.

17 Printed notice, signed B.P. Portal, Colonel Commanding Troops, Curragh, 13 Aug. 1915, by kind permission of the family.

18 Letter from Bertram to Melville, 1 Oct. 1915, HRO, 6A08/J2.

19 Report of the Royal Commission on the Rebellion in Ireland, Minutes of Evidence (HMSO,1916), 65.

20 Ibid, 22, 36 and 40; Letter from Bertram to Melville, 1 Oct. 1915, HRO, 6A08/J2.

21 R. Grayson, *Dublin's Great Wars: The First World War, the Easter Rising and the Irish Revolution* (Cambridge, 2018), 8-12.

22 Intelligence report about an armed rising in Ireland, 22 Mar. 1916, University College Dublin Library, https://doi.org/10.7925/drs1.ucdlib_53987, (Accessed 15 Feb. 2021.)

23 Unpublished transcript of the diary of Colonel Portal, 24 Apr. 1916, by kind permission of the family. 'Warned about a fortnight ago by G.O.C. that there was a chance of a rising attack so fortunately the Curragh officers were not on leave.'

24 L. O'Broin, *Dublin Castle and the 1916 Rising* (Letchworth, 1966), 10.

25 C. Costello, *A Most Delightful Station, the British Army on the Curragh of Kildare, 1855-1922* (Cork, 1999), 295.

26 Unpublished transcript of the diary of Major Sir Thomas Salt, by kind permission of Sir Michael Salt.

27 Letter from General French to the War Office, 2 May 1916, TNA, WO32/9575.

28 Unpublished transcript of the diary of Colonel Portal, 24 Apr.-21 May 1916, by kind permission of the family.

29 Unpublished transcript of the diary of Major Sir Thomas Salt, by kind permission of Sir Michael Salt.

30 The friendship between the two families endured. Sir Thomas Salt's son married Bertram's great-niece, Meriel Wiliams.

31 'A record of the Irish rebellion of 1916', *Irish Life,* 1916, Trinity College Dublin Library, Gall-TT-15-33_p22_WEB. (Accessed 18 Feb. 2021.)

32 Unpublished transcript of the diary of Major Sir Thomas Salt, by kind permission of Sir Michael Salt.

33 Unpublished transcript of the diary of Colonel Portal, 24 Apr. 1916, by kind permission of the family.

34 The local Dublin exchange at Crown Alley remained connected and was in British hands but communication was still not secure. S. Ferguson, 'Dublin's GPO Staff in 1916: A Neglected Story of Quiet Heroism', *American Journal of Irish Studies,* (14, 2017), 156.

35 Report of the Royal Commission on the Rebellion in Ireland, Minutes of Evidence (HMSO, 1916), 5 and 87.

36 J. Conolly, 'Street Fighting – Summary', *Workers' Republic*, 24 Jul. 1915. https://www.marxists.org/archive/connolly/1915/rw/stfight.htm. (Accessed 18 Feb. 2021.)

37 Unpublished transcript of the diary of Major Sir Thomas Salt, by kind permission of Sir Michael Salt; Unpublished transcript of the diary of Colonel Portal, 25 Apr. 1916, by kind permission of the family.

38 Unpublished transcript of the diary of Colonel Portal, 25 Apr. 1916, by kind permission of the family.

39 Ibid.

40 Sinn Féin Rebellion Handbook, (*Weekly Irish Times*, Dublin, 1917), 9.

41 *Elsie Mahaffy's diary*, Trinity College Archives, TCD MS 2074. 'Rachel and I climbed to the top storey of a house on the north side of the front Court to look up Sackville street to the Post Office, a memorable and dreadful sight.'

42 Report by Major Harris, adjutant, Dublin University OTC, May 1916, Trinity College Archives, TCD MS 2783/64.

43 *Elsie Mahaffy's diary,* Trinity College Archives, TCD MS 2074.

44 General French's dispatch on the Rebellion in Dublin, Supplement to the London Gazette, 21 Jul. 1916, 7309.

45 *Elsie Mahaffy's diary*, Trinity College Archives, TCD MS 2074.

46 Unpublished transcript of the diary of Colonel Portal, 25 Apr. 1916, by kind permission of the family.

47 Sinn Féin Rebellion Handbook, (*Weekly Irish Times*, Dublin, 1917), 23.

48 Unpublished transcript of the diary of Colonel Portal, 27 Apr. 1916, by kind permission of the family.

49 Typescript memoirs of Brigadier General Ernest Maconchy, 1860-1920, National Army Museum, NAM. 1979-08-62-1;

50 B. Campbell, B. Hughes and S. Schreibman, 'Contested Memories: revisiting the Battle of Mount Street Bridge, 1916', *British Journal for Military History*, 4,1 (2017), 14.

51 Unpublished transcript of the diary of Colonel Portal, 26 Apr. 1916, by kind permission of the family.

52 L. O'Broin, *Dublin Castle and the 1916 Rising* (New York, 1971), 110.

53 Rebellion in Ireland: summary of reports received up to 1pm on 26 April, TNA, WO 32/9510.

54 General French's dispatch on the Rebellion in Dublin, Supplement to the London Gazette, 21 Jul. 1916, 7310.

55 Unpublished transcript of the diary of Colonel Portal, 26 Apr. 1916, by kind permission of the family.

56 Bertram told his family that it was. Cecilia, his youngest daughter, is quoted in A. Pitcher, *A History of Overton* (Author, 1984), 51-2. 'He needed to move troops from one place to another and this was virtually impossible because of the stiff opposition. However, he had a marvelous idea. From the Guinness Brewery he acquired one of their large boilers, had it mounted on the back of a truck and then had slits cut into it so his men could fire through them.' A picture of the armoured vehicle in her book could only have come from Cecilia.

57 Guinness Archive Collection, GDB/CO04.03/0011.

58 H. H. P. Deasy was recruited to the regiment as a captain on 7 Aug. 1914, Army List, Nov. 1914, 8th Reserve Regiment of Cavalry, 175.

59 Unpublished transcript of Bertram Portal's Diary, Aug. 1901 to Jun. 1902, by kind permission of the family.

60 Deasy Motor Car Manufacturing Co., Grace's Guide to British Industrial

History. www.gracesguide.co.uk/Henry_Hugh_Peter_Deasy#cite_note-3. (Accessed 22 Feb. 2021.)

61 No records from the railway workshops have survived apart from the invoice. There is an often-repeated but very unlikely story that the design was by Colonel Henry Allett, a 69-year-old draft conducting officer attached to the 3rd Batt. Royal Irish Rifles in Dublin. Allatt was a poultry farmer from Farnham in Surrey who is not known to have designed vehicles of any sort. He was on in England leave when the uprising broke out and he could not have arrived back in Dublin in time.

62 Unpublished transcript of the diary of Major Sir Thomas Salt, by kind permission of Sir Michael Salt.

63 *Report by the Guinness chairman to shareholders, Jan. 1917*, Sinn Fein Rebellion Handbook, (*Weekly Irish Times*, Dublin, 1917), 28.

64 Churchill's concept of a 'land cruiser', later code-named 'water tank', was a platform for machine guns with the infantry following behind. M. Gilbert, *Churchill, A Life* (Derby, 1991), 293. It was top-secret and Portal could not have known of it.

65 Situation in Dublin about 1.15 on 27 April, TNA, WO 32/9510. 'Guinness had mounted boilers on motor lorries and loopholed them and these were conveying soldiers to points of vantage chiefly in Capel St.'

66 Unpublished transcript of the diary of Major Sir Thomas Salt, by kind permission of Sir Michael Salt.

67 Photocopied pages from 2/6th Bn Sherwood Foresters history, covering their service in Ireland during the 1916 Rebellion, National Army Museum, 1994-02-73.

68 Unpublished transcript of the diary of Major Sir Thomas Salt, by kind permission of Sir Michael Salt.

69 Unpublished transcript of the diary of Colonel Portal, 27 Apr. 1916, by kind permission of the family.

70 General French's dispatch on the Rebellion in Dublin, Supplement to the London Gazette, 21 Jul. 1916, 7309.

71 Unpublished transcript of the diary of Major Sir Thomas Salt, by kind permission of Sir Michael Salt.

72   Ibid.

73   Interview with the Daily Mail, 18 May 1916, quoted in Sinn Fein Rebellion Handbook, (*Weekly Irish Times*, Dublin, 1917), 23.

74   Unpublished transcript of the diary of Colonel Portal, 28 Apr. 1916, by kind permission of the family.

75   Typescript copy of a message from Lt. Col. R. L. Owen, 3rd Battalion, Royal Irish Regiment, 29 Apr. 1916, National Library of Ireland, vtls000652440.

76   Unpublished transcript of the diary of Colonel Portal, 28 Apr. 1916, by kind permission of the family.

77   Account of the Easter Rising by Elizabeth O'Farrell, National Library of Ireland, MS 50, 246/5/1.

78   Unpublished transcript of the diary of Colonel Portal, 28 Apr. 1916, by kind permission of the family.

79   Scheme for further operations to cope with the rebellion in the Dublin District Area, University College Dublin Archive, https://doi.org/10.7925/drs1.ucdlib_54003. (Accessed 26 Feb. 2021.)

80   Unpublished transcript of the diary of Colonel Portal, 29 Apr.-2 May 1916, by kind permission of the family.

81   General French's dispatch on the Easter Rising, Supplement to the *London Gazette*, 21 Jul. 1916, 7311.

82   Maxwell to Lord French, 29 Apr. 1916. University College Dublin Archive, https://doi.org/10.7925/drs1.ucdlib_54001. (Accessed 26 Feb. 2021.)

83   General Maxwell, telegram to London, 10 May 1916, University College Dublin Library, 54033.

84   Unpublished transcript of the diary of Colonel Portal, 5 May 1916, by kind permission of the family.

85   Ibid.

86   Unpublished transcript of the diary of Major Sir Thomas Salt, by kind permission of Sir Michael Salt.

87   Castlebar prison records, https://portwest.mde.ie/westport1619/castlebar-prison-record. (Accessed 20 Feb. 2021.)

88   Unpublished transcript of the diary of Colonel Portal, 5 May 1916, by kind permission of the family.

89 D. Figgis, *Recollections of the Irish War* (New York, undated, *c.*1925), 21-58.

90 Castlebar Prison records, https://portwest.mde.ie/westport1619/castlebar-prison-record. (Accessed 20 Feb. 2021.)

91 Memorandum sent from Castlebar, 14 May 1916, National Archives, Dublin. Reproduced in https://portwest.mde.ie/westport1619/2016/03/15/memo-sent-by-colonel-b-p-portal-in-castlebar-to-head-quarters. (Accessed 18 Feb. 2021.)

92 Letter from Bertram to Melville, 14 May 1916, HRO, 6A08/J2.

93 Unpublished transcript of the diary of Colonel Portal, 18-22 May 1916, by kind permission of the family.

94 Cabinet Papers, Ireland, 1916, TNA, CAB 38/147/13.

95 Letter from General Maxwell to Field Marshal Lord French, 30 Apr. 1916, University College Dublin Library, 54007.

96 General Maxwell, draft dispatch, 23 May 1916, TNA, WO32/9523.

97 General French's dispatch on the Easter Rising, Supplement to the London Gazette, 21 Jul. 1916, 7307-12.

98 Cabinet papers, 15 May 1916, TNA, CAB 37/147/38.

99 *The Times*, 25 Jan. 1917.

100 Letter from Margaret to Melville, undated, HRO, 6A08/J4.

101 M. Norway, *The Sinn Fein Rebellion as I saw it* (London, 1916), 14-15; 37-41; The personal experience of Miss L. Stokes during the Sinn Féin Rebellion of 1916, Trinity College Dublin Library, TCD MS 11507.

102 Sinn Féin Rebellion Handbook, (*Weekly Irish Times*, Dublin, 1917), 69.

103 C. Townshend, *The Republic: the Fight for Irish Independence 1918-1923*, (Penguin, U.K., 2014), 219 and 283*; Westminster Gazette,* 11 May 1921.

104 Obituary, *Hampshire Chronicle*, 12 Feb. 1949.

CHAPTER 8: THE WESTERN FRONT

1 M. Gilbert, *Churchill, A Life* (London, 1991), 143.

2 *ODNB,* H.H. Kitchener.

3 J. Boff and W. Philpot, 'Transforming War, 1914-1918', *British Journal for Military History,* 5,2 (2019), passim.

4   Aerial reconnaissance and tactical bombing, radio, gas and deep tunneled mines.

5   Letter from Bertram to Melville, 30 May 1916, by kind permission of the family.

6   Letter from Mittie to Melville, 30 Jun. 1916, HRO, 6A/08/J1.

7   Ibid, 28 May 1917, HRO, 6A/08/J4.

8   Letter from Bertram to Melville, 30 May 1916, by kind permission of the family.

9   Diary of Brig. Gen. Bertram Portal, covering service as a Cavalry Brigade Commander on the Western Front between Jun. 1916 and Apr. 1917, National Army Museum, 2008-07-17.

10 Ibid.

11 Ibid.

12 Letter from Mittie to Bertram, 12 Nov. 1917, by kind permission of the family.

13 D. Kenyon, *Horsemen in No-Man's Land* (Barnsley, 2011), 86-132.

14 War Diary, 3rd Cavalry Division, Apr. 1917, TNA, WO 95/1141/3.

15 War Diary, 7th Cavalry Brigade, Apr. 1917, TNA, WO 95/1154/2.

16 J. Nicholls, *Cheerful Sacrifice: the Battle of Arras 1917* (Barnsley, 2005), 210-11.

17 R. Grayson. 'A Life in the Trenches: The Use of Operation War Diary and Crowdsourcing Methods to Provide an Understanding of the British Army's Day-to-Day Life on the Western Front', *British Journal for Military History*, 2,2, (2016), passim.

18 Letter from Bertram to Melville, 7 May 1918, HRO, 6A08/J4.

19 *Hants & Berks Gazette*, 5 May 1917.

20 D. Kenyon, *Horsemen in No-Man's Land* (Barnsley, 2011), 185-200.

21 G. Micholls, *A history of the 17th Lancers, 1895 – 1924* (London, 1931), 116-125.

22 War Diary, 7th Cavalry Brigade, Mar.-Apr. 1918, TNA, WO 95/1154/1/3.

23 War Diary, 3rd Cavalry Division, TNA, WO95/1142/5/1.

24 War Diary, 3rd Cavalry Division, TNA, WO95/1141/4/1.

25 G. Micholls, *A history of the 17th Lancers, 1895 – 1924* (London, 1931), 125.

26 War Diary, 7th Cavalry Brigade, TNA, WO95/1154/1/3.

27 Letter from Mittie to Melville, 24 Mar. 1918, HRO, 6A08/J4.

28 War Diary, 3rd Cavalry Division, TNA, WO95/1141/4/1.

29 Letter from Mittie to Melville, 30 Mar. 1918, HRO, 6A08/J4.

30 Ibid.

31 *Hants & Berks Gazette*, 1 Jun. 1918.

CHAPTER 9: A LONG RETIREMENT

1   Letter from 'Nan' Jagg to Melville, 1 Nov. 1918, HRO, 196A08/J8.

2   Letter from Charlotte to Melville, 10 Nov. 1918, HRO, 6A08/J7.

3   Letter from Margaret to Melville, 10 Nov. 1918, HRO, 6A08/J7.

4   Letter from Charlotte to Melville, 10 Nov. 1918, HRO, 6A08/J7.

5   Letter from Bertram to Melville, 12 Nov. 1918, HRO, 6A08/J2.

6   *Hants & Berks Gazette*, 8 Mar. 1919; Ibid, 24 Jul. 1920.

7   Ibid, 25 Jan. 1919.

8   Ibid.

9   *Hampshire Chronicle,* 2 Apr. 1898.

10 *Hants & Berks Gazette,* 28 Dec. 1923.

11 Ibid, 26 Jul. 1919; *Hampshire Independent*, 15 Feb. 1919.

12 *Hampshire Advertiser*, 3 Jul. 1920.

13 Enham Trust, www.enhamtrust.org.uk/Pages/FAQs/Category/history

14 *Hampshire Advertiser*, 3 Jul. 1920.

15 *A.* Pitcher, *A History of Overton* (Author, 1984), 57.

16 *Hampshire Advertiser*, 3 May 1919; Ibid, 28 Feb.1920; Ibid, 2 Jun. 1920.

17 Ibid, 14 Mar. 1925.

18 *Hants & Berks Gazette*, 5 May 1921.

19 Sir Francis Portal, *Portals* (Oxford, 1962), 92.

20 Company Minute book, 1920-1929, HRO, 132M98/A5/1.

21 Kelly's Directory, Overton, 1927; Sir Francis Portal, *Portals*, (Oxford, 1962), 93.

22 *Staffordshire Advertiser*, 23 Dec. 1926.

23 *Hants & Berks Gazette*, 4 May 1929.

24 Ibid, 11 Jan. 1930.

25   Ibid, 24 Sept. 1937.

26   Obituary, *Hampshire Chronicle*, 12 Feb. 1949.

27   *Hants & Berks Gazette*, 28 Nov. 1940.

28   Obituary, *Hampshire Chronicle*, 12 Feb. 1949.

29   Recounted by Simon Portal, Miscellaneous papers of Bertram Portal, 1940s, HRO, 6A08/E5.

30   *Bath Echo*, https://www.bathecho.co.uk/news/bath-remembers-devastating-1942-blitz-bombing. (Accessed 2 Feb. 2021)

31   Letter from the manager of the Francis Hotel, Bath to Bertram, HRO, 6A08/E5.

32   *Hants & Berks Gazette*, 13 Sept. 1943.

33   Ibid, 31 Dec. 1943.

34   *Hampshire Chronicle*, 17 Feb. 1945.

35   John Litchfield's diary, contributed by Mark Litchfield.

36   Ibid.

37   *Hampshire Chronicle,* 17 Feb. 1945.

38   *Hants & Berks Gazette,* 21 Sept. 1945; Ibid, 26 Oct. 1945.

39   Ibid, 11 Feb. 1949.

40   Obituary, *Hampshire Chronicle*, 12 Feb. 1949.

POSTSCRIPT

1   L. James, *Raj, the Making and Unmaking of British India* (Great Britain, 1997), 309.

BIBLOGRAPHY

PRIMARY SOURCES

BRITISH LIBRARY

Letters from Bertram Percy Portal to his mother, 1896-1898, Mss Eur F494.

HAMPSHIRE RECORD OFFICE (HAMPSHIRE ARCHIVES)

Letters and miscellaneous papers of (Brig-Gen Sir) Bertram Percy Portal, 1866-1910, 6A08/E2.

Letters to (Brig-Gen Sir) Bertram Percy Portal from Douglas Haig (later Field Marshal, Sir Douglas Haig) and related papers, 1904-1928, 6A08/E3.

Miscellaneous papers of (Brig-Gen Sir) Bertram Percy Portal, 1910s-1940s, 6A08/E4.

Miscellaneous papers of (Brig-Gen Sir) Bertram Percy Portal, 1940s, 6A08/E5.

Letters to Melville Edward Bertram Portal from his mother Margaret Portal, 1901-1918, 6A08/J1.

Letters to Melville Edward Bertram Portal from his father Bertram Portal, 1903-1918, 6A08/J2.

Letters to Melville Edward Bertram Portal from his parents in India, 1905-1907, 6A08/J3.

Letters to Melville Edward Bertram Portal from his sisters, c1910-1918, 6A08/J7.

Letters to Melville Edward Bertram Portal from 'Nan' Jagg, Nanny to the whole family, 1909-1919, 6A08/J8

Diary of Margaret Portal, in Capetown, 6A08/F3

THE NATIONAL ARCHIVES, KEW

OVERSEAS: Ireland: 1916 Rebellion: reports, summaries of events, WO 32/9510.

War Diary, 3rd Cavalry Division, April 1917, TNA, WO 95/1141/3.

War Diary, 3rd Cavalry Division, 1st Mar.-31st Jul.,1918, TNA, WO 95/1142/5.

War Diary, 7th Cavalry Brigade, TNA, WO 95/1154/1.

NATIONAL ARMY MUSEUM

Transcribed typed extracts from the diaries of Maj (Later Brig Gen) Bertram Percy Portal DSO covering service with the 17th Lancers in the Boer War, February to September 1900 and as a Cavalry Brigade Commander on the Western Front between Jun 1916 and Apr 1917, 2008-07-17.

TRINITY COLLEGE DUBLIN ARCHIVES

Changed Utterly, https://www.tcd.ie/library/1916/

UNIVERSITY COLLEGE DUBLIN LIBRARY

Éamon de Valera Papers: British documents relating to 1916, https://doi.org/10.7925/drs1.ucdlib _53985.

THE LONDON GAZETTE

Report of the Royal Commission on the Rebellion in Ireland, Minutes of Evidence, (H.M.S.O.,1916).

General French's dispatch on the Easter Rising, Supplement to the London Gazette, 21 Jul. 1916, 7308.

NEWSPAPERS

The British Newspaper Archive https://www.britishnewspaperarchive.co.uk/
Hants & Berks Gazette
The Times Archive

SECONDARY SOURCES

Churchill, W. S., *Ian Hamilton's March* (London, 1900).
Churchill, W. S., *My Early Life* (London, 1947).
Costello, C., *A Most Delightful Station, The British Army on the Curragh of Kildare, 1855-1922* (Cork, 1999).
Fortescue, J.W., *A History of the 17th Lancers* (London, 1895).
Grayson, R., *Dublin's Great Wars: The First World War, the Easter Rising and the Irish Revolution* (Cambridge, 2018).
Micholls, G., *A History of the 17th Lancers, 1895-1923* (London, 1931).
Mockler Ferryman, A.F., *Annals of Sandhurst* (London, 1900).
Packenham, T., *The Boer War* (London,1979).
Pitcher, A., *A History of Overton* (Author, 1984).
Portal, Sir Francis, *Portals* (Oxford, 1962).
Townsend, C., *Easter 1916: the Irish Rebellion* (London, 2005).
Waldram, R. *et al*, *A History of Overton from 1500* (Heritage Overton, 2019).

INDEX

 Matador